CONNECTED MATHEM

Looking for Pythagoras

The Pythagorean Theorem

Glenda Lappan, Elizabeth Difanis Phillips,
James T. Fey, Susan N. Friel

PEARSON

Boston, Massachusetts • Chandler, Arizona • Glenview, Illinois • Hoboken, New Jersey

Connected Mathematics® was developed at Michigan State University with financial support from the Michigan State University Office of the Provost, Computing and Technology, and the College of Natural Science.

This material is based upon work supported by the National Science Foundation under Grant No. MDR 9150217 and Grant No. ESI 9986372. Opinions expressed are those of the authors and not necessarily those of the Foundation.

As with prior editions of this work, the authors and administration of Michigan State University preserve a tradition of devoting royalties from this publication to support activities sponsored by the MSU Mathematics Education Enrichment Fund.

PEARSON

Authors

A Team of Experts

Glenda Lappan is a University Distinguished Professor in the Program in Mathematics Education (PRIME) and the Department of Mathematics at Michigan State University. Her research and development interests are in the connected areas of students' learning of mathematics and mathematics teachers' professional growth and change related to the development and enactment of K–12 curriculum materials.

Elizabeth Difanis Phillips is a Senior Academic Specialist in the Program in Mathematics Education (PRIME) and the Department of Mathematics at Michigan State University. She is interested in teaching and learning mathematics for both teachers and students. These interests have led to curriculum and professional development projects at the middle school and high school levels, as well as projects related to the teaching and learning of algebra across the grades.

James T. Fey is a Professor Emeritus at the University of Maryland. His consistent professional interest has been development and research focused on curriculum materials that engage middle and high school students in problem-based collaborative investigations of mathematical ideas and their applications.

Susan N. Friel is a Professor of Mathematics Education in the School of Education at the University of North Carolina at Chapel Hill. Her research interests focus on statistics education for middle-grade students and, more broadly, on teachers' professional development and growth in teaching mathematics K–8.

With... Yvonne Grant and Jacqueline Stewart

Yvonne Grant teaches mathematics at Portland Middle School in Portland, Michigan. Jacqueline Stewart is a recently retired high school teacher of mathematics at Okemos High School in Okemos, Michigan. Both Yvonne and Jacqueline have worked on a variety of activities related to the development, implementation, and professional development of the CMP curriculum since its beginning in 1991.

Development Team

CMP3 Authors

Glenda Lappan, University Distinguished Professor, Michigan State University
Elizabeth Difanis Phillips, Senior Academic Specialist, Michigan State University
James T. Fey, Professor Emeritus, University of Maryland
Susan N. Friel, Professor, University of North Carolina – Chapel Hill

With...
Yvonne Grant, Portland Middle School, Michigan
Jacqueline Stewart, Mathematics Consultant, Mason, Michigan

In Memory of... William M. Fitzgerald, Professor (Deceased), Michigan State University, who made substantial contributions to conceptualizing and creating CMP1.

Administrative Assistant

Michigan State University
Judith Martus Miller

Support Staff

Michigan State University
Undergraduate Assistants:
Bradley Robert Corlett, Carly Fleming,
Erin Lucian, Scooter Nowak

Development Assistants

Michigan State University
Graduate Research Assistants:
Richard "Abe" Edwards, Nic Gilbertson,
Funda Gonulates, Aladar Horvath,
Eun Mi Kim, Kevin Lawrence, Jennifer
Nimtz, Joanne Philhower, Sasha Wang

Assessment Team

Maine
Falmouth Public Schools
Falmouth Middle School: Shawn Towle

Michigan
Ann Arbor Public Schools
Tappan Middle School
Anne Marie Nicoll-Turner

Portland Public Schools
Portland Middle School
Holly DeRosia, Yvonne Grant

Traverse City Area Public Schools
Traverse City East Middle School
Jane Porath, Mary Beth Schmitt

Traverse City West Middle School
Jennifer Rundio, Karrie Tufts

Ohio
Clark-Shawnee Local Schools
Rockway Middle School: Jim Mamer

Content Consultants

Michigan State University
Peter Lappan, Professor Emeritus,
Department of Mathematics

Normandale Community College
Christopher Danielson, Instructor,
Department of Mathematics & Statistics

University of North Carolina – Wilmington
Dargan Frierson, Jr., Professor, Department
of Mathematics & Statistics

Student Activities
Michigan State University
Brin Keller, Associate Professor,
Department of Mathematics

Consultants

Indiana

Purdue University
Mary Bouck, Mathematics Consultant

Michigan

Oakland Schools
Valerie Mills, Mathematics Education Supervisor
Mathematics Education Consultants:
Geraldine Devine, Dana Gosen

Ellen Bacon, Independent Mathematics Consultant

New York

University of Rochester
Jeffrey Choppin, Associate Professor

Ohio

University of Toledo
Debra Johanning, Associate Professor

Pennsylvania

University of Pittsburgh
Margaret Smith, Professor

Texas

University of Texas at Austin
Emma Trevino, Supervisor of Mathematics Programs, The Dana Center

Mathematics for All Consulting
Carmen Whitman, Mathematics Consultant

....

Reviewers

Michigan

Ionia Public Schools
Kathy Dole, Director of Curriculum and Instruction

Grand Valley State University
Lisa Kasmer, Assistant Professor

Portland Public Schools
Teri Keusch, Classroom Teacher

Minnesota

Hopkins School District 270
Michele Luke, Mathematics Coordinator

....

Field Test Sites for CMP3

Michigan

Ann Arbor Public Schools
Tappan Middle School
Anne Marie Nicoll-Turner*

Portland Public Schools
Portland Middle School: Mark Braun,
Angela Buckland, Holly DeRosia,
Holly Feldpausch, Angela Foote,
Yvonne Grant*, Kristin Roberts,
Angie Stump, Tammi Wardwell

Traverse City Area Public Schools
Traverse City East Middle School
Ivanka Baic Berkshire, Brenda Dunscombe,
Tracie Herzberg, Deb Larimer, Jan Palkowski,
Rebecca Perreault, Jane Porath*,
Robert Sagan, Mary Beth Schmitt*

Traverse City West Middle School
Pamela Alfieri, Jennifer Rundio,
Maria Taplin, Karrie Tufts*

Maine

Falmouth Public Schools
Falmouth Middle School: Sally Bennett,
Chris Driscoll, Sara Jones, Shawn Towle*

Minnesota

Minneapolis Public Schools
Jefferson Community School
Leif Carlson*,
Katrina Hayek Munsisoumang*

Ohio

Clark-Shawnee Local Schools
Reid School: Joanne Gilley
Rockway Middle School: Jim Mamer*
Possum School: Tami Thomas

*Indicates a Field Test Site Coordinator

Looking for Pythagoras

The Pythagorean Theorem

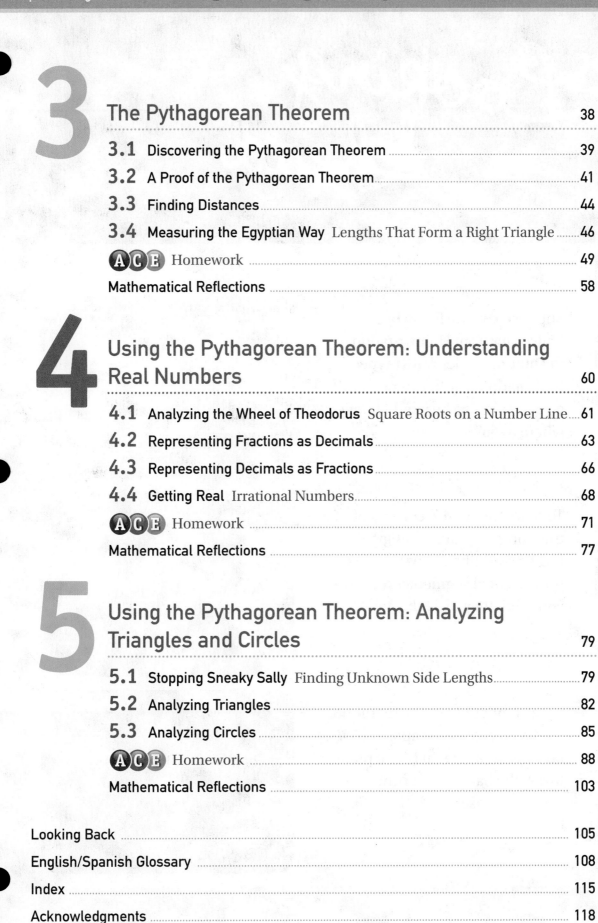

Looking Ahead

Suppose you are flying by helicopter from Union Station to Dupont Circle. **What** types of information would you need to give the pilot so he would know where to go?

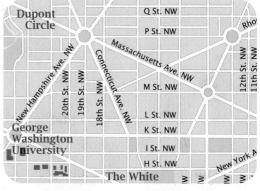

To mark the square corners of their property, ancient Egyptians used a rope divided with knots into 12 equal segments. **How** do you think they used this tool?

On a standard baseball diamond, the bases are 90 feet apart. **How** far must a catcher at home plate throw the ball to get a runner out at second base?

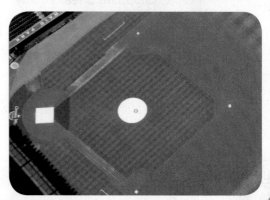

In this Unit, you will explore side lengths and areas of right triangles and squares. Your explorations will lead you to discover one of the most important relationships in all of mathematics: the *Pythagorean Theorem*. The Pythagorean Theorem is so important that much of geometry, trigonometry, and calculus would be impossible without it.

In earlier *Connected Mathematics* Units, you used whole numbers and fractions to describe lengths. In *Looking for Pythagoras,* you will work with lengths that are impossible to describe with whole numbers or fractions. To talk about such lengths, you need to use another type of number, called an *irrational number*.

The skills you develop in this Unit will help you answer questions like those on the facing page.

Mathematical Highlights

Looking for Pythagoras

In *Looking for Pythagoras,* you will explore an important relationship among the side lengths of a right triangle.

You will learn how to

- Develop strategies for finding the distance between two points on a coordinate grid

- Explain a proof of the Pythagorean Theorem

- Understand and use the Pythagorean Theorem to solve everyday problems

- Write fractions as repeating or terminating decimals

- Write decimals as fractions

- Recognize rational and irrational numbers

- Locate irrational numbers on a number line

- Relate the area of a square to its side length, and the volume of a cube to its side length

- Estimate square roots and cube roots

When you encounter a new problem, it is a good idea to ask yourself questions. In this Unit, you might ask questions such as:

What are the quantities in this problem?

Is the Pythagorean Theorem useful and appropriate in this situation?

How do I know?

Do I need to find the distance between two points?

How are the side length and the area of a square related?

How can I estimate the square root or cube root of a number?

Mathematical Practices and Habits of Mind

In the *Connected Mathematics* curriculum you will develop an understanding of important mathematical ideas by solving problems and reflecting on the mathematics involved. Every day, you will use "habits of mind" to make sense of problems and apply what you learn to new situations. Some of these habits are described by the *Common Core State Standards for Mathematical Practices* (MP).

MP1 Make sense of problems and persevere in solving them.

When using mathematics to solve a problem, it helps to think carefully about

- data and other facts you are given and what additional information you need to solve the problem;
- strategies you have used to solve similar problems and whether you could solve a related simpler problem first;
- how you could express the problem with equations, diagrams, or graphs;
- whether your answer makes sense.

MP2 Reason abstractly and quantitatively.

When you are asked to solve a problem, it often helps to

- focus first on the key mathematical ideas;
- check that your answer makes sense in the problem setting;
- use what you know about the problem setting to guide your mathematical reasoning.

MP3 Construct viable arguments and critique the reasoning of others.

When you are asked to explain why a conjecture is correct, you can

- show some examples that fit the claim and explain why they fit;
- show how a new result follows logically from known facts and principles.

When you believe a mathematical claim is incorrect, you can

- show one or more counterexamples—cases that don't fit the claim;
- find steps in the argument that do not follow logically from prior claims.

MP4 Model with mathematics.

When you are asked to solve problems, it often helps to

- think carefully about the numbers or geometric shapes that are the most important factors in the problem, then ask yourself how those factors are related to each other;
- express data and relationships in the problem with tables, graphs, diagrams, or equations, and check your result to see if it makes sense.

MP5 Use appropriate tools strategically.

When working on mathematical questions, you should always

- decide which tools are most helpful for solving the problem and why;
- try a different tool when you get stuck.

MP6 Attend to precision.

In every mathematical exploration or problem-solving task, it is important to

- think carefully about the required accuracy of results; is a number estimate or geometric sketch good enough, or is a precise value or drawing needed?
- report your discoveries with clear and correct mathematical language that can be understood by those to whom you are speaking or writing.

MP7 Look for and make use of structure.

In mathematical explorations and problem solving, it is often helpful to

- look for patterns that show how data points, numbers, or geometric shapes are related to each other;
- use patterns to make predictions.

MP8 Look for and express regularity in repeated reasoning.

When results of a repeated calculation show a pattern, it helps to

- express that pattern as a general rule that can be used in similar cases;
- look for shortcuts that will make the calculation simpler in other cases.

You will use all of the Mathematical Practices in this Unit. Sometimes, when you look at a Problem, it is obvious which practice is most helpful. At other times, you will decide on a practice to use during class explorations and discussions. After completing each Problem, ask yourself:

- What mathematics have I learned by solving this Problem?
- What Mathematical Practices were helpful in learning this mathematics?

Coordinate Grids

In this Investigation, you will use a coordinate grid to locate points on the plane. You will then explore how to find distances between points and areas of figures on a coordinate grid.

In the first two Problems of this Investigation, the coordinate grid is in the form of a street map of a fictional city called Euclid. The streets in most cities do not form perfect coordinate grids as they do in Euclid. However, many cities have streets that are loosely based on a coordinate system. One well-known example is Washington, D.C.

....

Common Core State Standards

Essential for 8.G.B.6 Explain a proof of the Pythagorean Theorem and its converse.

Essential for 8.G.B.8 Apply the Pythagorean Theorem to find the distance between two points in a coordinate system.

The map on the next page shows the central part of Washington, D.C. The city's street system was designed by Pierre L'Enfant in 1791.

L'Enfant's design is based on a coordinate system. Here are some key features of L'Enfant's system:

- The north-south and east-west streets form grid lines.

- The origin is at the Capitol.

- The vertical axis is formed by North and South Capitol Streets.

- The horizontal axis is the line stretching from the Lincoln Memorial, through the Mall, and down East Capitol Street.

- The axes divide the city into four quadrants known as Northeast (NE), Northwest (NW), Southwest (SW), and Southeast (SE).

- Describe the locations of these landmarks:

    George Washington University

    Dupont Circle

    Benjamin Banneker Park

    The White House

    Union Station

- How can you find the distance from Union Station to Dupont Circle?

- Find the intersection of G Street and 8th Street SE and the intersection of G Street and 8th Street NW. How are these locations related to the U.S. Capitol Building?

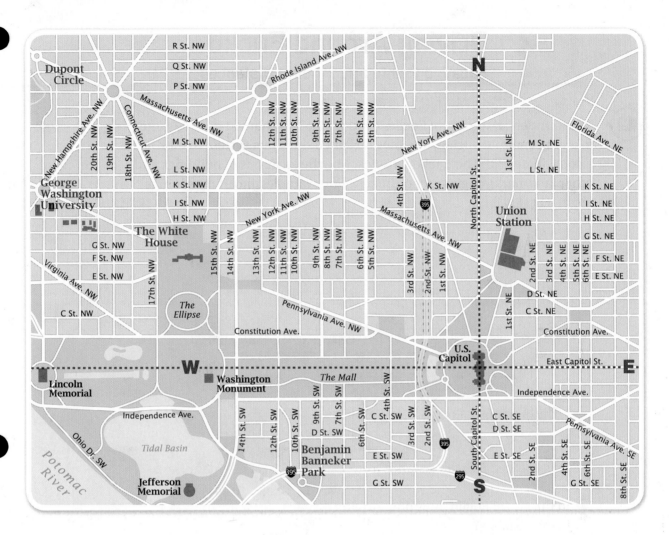

In mathematics, you use a coordinate system to describe the locations of points. Recall that horizontal and vertical number lines, called the *x*- and *y*-axes, divide the plane into four quadrants.

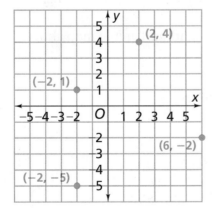

You describe the location of a point by giving its coordinates as an ordered pair of the form (*x*, *y*). The coordinate grid above shows four points labeled with their coordinates. For example, the point (−2, −5) is 2 units to the left and 5 units below the origin.

1.1 Driving Around Euclid
Locating Points and Finding Distances

The founders of the city of Euclid loved math. They named their city after a famous mathematician, and they designed the street system to look like a coordinate grid. The Euclideans describe the locations of buildings and other landmarks by giving coordinates. For example, the art museum is located at (6, 1).

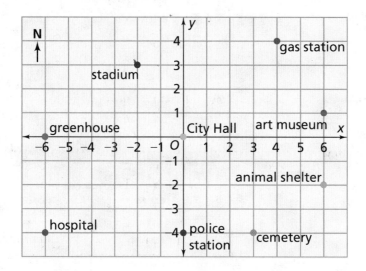

- In the city of Euclid, how does driving distance compare to flying distance?

Problem 1.1

Ⓐ Give the coordinates of each landmark in the map above.

1. gas station
2. animal shelter
3. stadium

Problem **1.1** *continued*

B Euclid's chief of police is planning emergency routes. She needs to find the shortest route between the following pairs of locations:

Pair 1: the police station to City Hall

Pair 2: the hospital to City Hall

Pair 3: the hospital to the art museum

   1. Give precise directions for an emergency car route for each pair.

   2. For each pair, find the total distance in blocks a police car following your route would travel.

C **1.** The stadium is at $(-2, 3)$ and the high school is at $(1, 8)$. What is the shortest driving distance (in blocks) between these two locations? Can you figure this out without looking at the grid? Explain.

   2. Suppose you know the coordinates of two landmarks in Euclid. How can you determine the shortest driving distance (in blocks) between them?

D **1.** A helicopter can travel directly from one point to another. For each pair in Question B, find the approximate distance (in blocks) a helicopter would have to travel to get from the starting location to the ending location. You may find it helpful to use a centimeter ruler.

   2. Will a direct helicopter route between two locations always be shorter than a car route? Explain your reasoning.

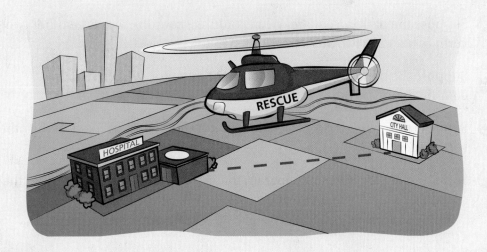

A C E Homework starts on page 14.

1.2 Planning Parks
Shapes on a Coordinate Grid

The Euclid City Council is developing parks with geometric shapes. For some of the parks, the council gives the park designers constraints. For example, Descartes Park must have corners at vertices (1, 1) and (4, 2).

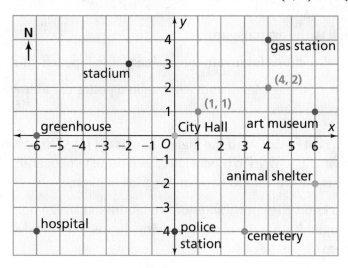

- What information do you need to show that the shape made by connecting four vertices is a square?

Problem 1.2

For each Question, explain how you know Descartes Park is the given shape.

A Suppose the park is a square. What could the coordinates of the other two vertices be? Give two answers.

B Suppose the park is a rectangle that is not a square. What could the coordinates of the other two vertices be?

C Suppose the park is a right triangle. What could the coordinates of the other vertex be?

D Suppose the park is a parallelogram that is not a rectangle. What could the coordinates of the other two vertices be?

A C E Homework starts on page 14.

1.3 Finding Areas

Below are some park designs submitted to the Euclid City Council. To determine costs, the council needs to know the area of each park.

 1.

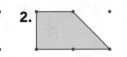 2.

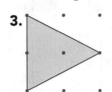 3.

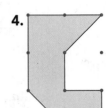 4.

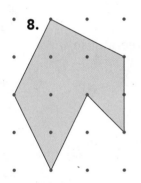 5.

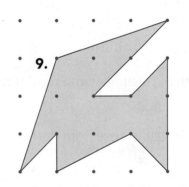 6.

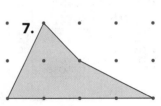 7.

8.

9.

10.

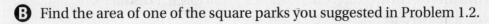

- How might you find the areas of irregular figures on dot paper?

Problem 1.3

Consider the horizontal or vertical distance between two adjacent dots to be 1 unit.

A Find the area of each figure.

B Find the area of one of the square parks you suggested in Problem 1.2.

C Describe the strategies you used in Questions A and B.

A C E Homework starts on page 14.

Applications

For Exercises 1–7, use the map of Euclid from Problem 1.1.

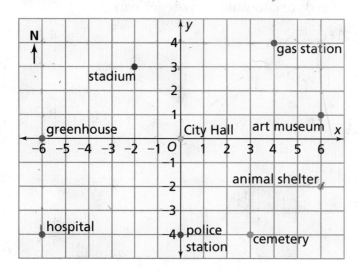

1. Give the coordinates of each landmark.

   a. art museum   **b.** hospital   **c.** greenhouse

2. What is the shortest driving distance from the animal shelter to the stadium?

3. What is the shortest driving distance from the hospital to the gas station?

4. Suppose you travel by taxi. What are the coordinates of a point halfway from City Hall to the hospital? Is there more than one possibility? Explain.

5. Suppose you traveled by helicopter. What are the coordinates of a point halfway from City Hall to the hospital? Is there more than one possibility? Explain.

6. **a.** Which landmarks are 7 blocks from City Hall by car?

   b. Give precise driving directions from City Hall to each landmark you listed in part (a).

7. Euclid Middle School is located at the intersection of two streets. The school is the same driving distance from the gas station as the hospital is from the greenhouse.

    a. List the coordinates of each place on the map where the school might be located.

    b. Find the flying distance (in blocks) from the gas station to each location you listed in part (a).

The points (0, 0) and (3, 2) are two vertices of a polygon with integer coordinates.

8. Suppose the polygon is a square. What could the other two vertices be?

9. Suppose the polygon is a nonrectangular parallelogram. What could the other two vertices be?

10. Suppose the polygon is a right triangle. What could the other vertex be?

The points (3, 3) and (2, 6) are two vertices of a right triangle. Use this information for Exercises 11–13.

11. Multiple Choice Which point could be the third vertex of the right triangle?

    A. $(3, 2)$ **B.** $(-1, 5)$ **C.** $(7, 4)$ **D.** $(0, 3)$

12. Give the coordinates of at least two other points that could be the third vertex.

13. How many right triangles with vertices (3, 3) and (2, 6) can you draw? Explain.

14. Can you connect the following points to form a parallelogram? Explain.

    $(1, 1)$ $(2, -2)$ $(4, 2)$ $(3, 5)$

Find the area of each triangle. If necessary, copy the triangles onto dot paper.

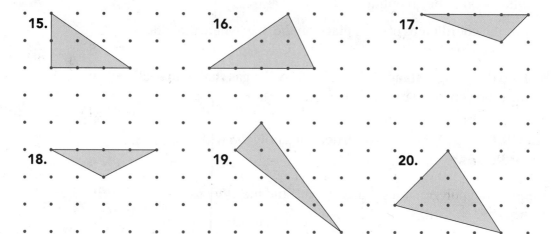

15.   16.   17.

18.   19.   20.

Find the area of each figure. Describe the method you use. If necessary, copy the figures onto dot paper.

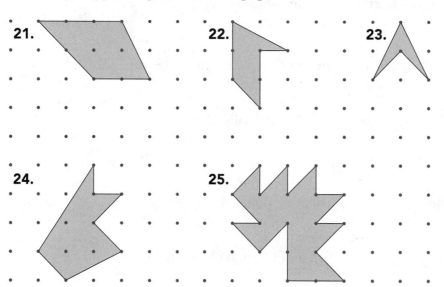

21.   22.   23.

24.   25.

● Connections

In the city of Euclid, the length of each block is 150 meters. Use this information and the map from Problem 1.1 for Exercises 26–28.

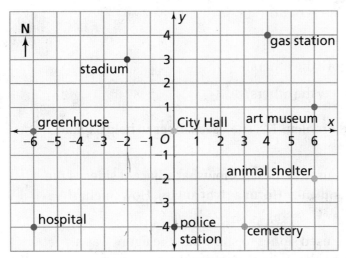

26. What is the shortest driving distance, in meters, from City Hall to the animal shelter?

27. What is the shortest driving distance, in meters, from the police station to the gas station?

28. Between which two landmarks is the shortest driving distance 750 meters?

For Exercises 29–33, use the map of Euclid from Problem 1.1.

29. Matsu walks 2 blocks west from the police station and then walks 3 blocks north. Give the coordinates of the place where he stops.

30. Amy is at City Hall. She wants to meet Matsu at his ending location from Exercise 29. What is the shortest route she can take if she walks along city streets? Is there more than one possible shortest route?

31. Simon leaves the stadium and walks 3 blocks east, then 3 blocks south, then 2 blocks west, and finally 4 blocks north. Give the coordinates of the place where he stops.

32. Aida wants to meet Simon at his ending location from Exercise 31. She is at City Hall. What is the shortest route she can take if she walks along city streets? Is there more than one possible shortest route?

33. In general, how can you use coordinates to find the shortest walking route from City Hall to any point in Euclid?

34. Refer to the ordered pairs below. Do *not* plot the points on a grid to answer the questions. Explain each answer.

$(2, -3)$	$(3, -4)$	$(-4, -5)$	$(4, 5)$
$(-4, 6)$	$(-5, -5)$	$(0, -6)$	$(6, 0)$

  a. Which point is farthest right?

  b. Which point is farthest left?

  c. Which point is above the others?

  d. Which point is below the others?

35. When Fabiola solved Problem 1.2, she used slopes to help explain her answers.

  a. In Question A, she used slopes to show that adjacent sides of the figure were **perpendicular** (form a right angle). How might she have done this?

  b. In Question D, she used slopes to show that the figure was a parallelogram. How might she have done this?

36. Below are equations for eight lines.

  line 1: $y = 3x + 5$ line 2: $y = 0.5x + 3$

  line 3: $y = 10 - 2x$ line 4: $y = 1 - \frac{1}{3}x$

  line 5: $y = 7 + 3x$ line 6: $y = -2x + 1$

  line 7: $y = 5 + 6x$ line 8: $y = 3x$

  a. Which of the lines are parallel to each other?

  b. Which of the lines are perpendicular to each other?

37. Marcia finds the area of a figure on dot paper by dividing it into smaller shapes. She finds the area of each smaller shape and writes the sum of the areas as $\frac{1}{2} \cdot 3 + \frac{1}{2} + \frac{1}{2} + 1$.

  a. What is the total area of the figure?

  b. On dot paper, draw a possible picture of the figure.

38. In the figure, a circle is inscribed in a square.

    a. Find the area of the circle.

    b. Find the area of the shaded region.

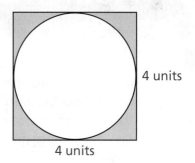

4 units

4 units

Extensions

39. Find a road map of your city or county. Figure out how to use the map's index to locate a city, street, or other landmark. How is finding a landmark by using an index description similar to and different from finding a landmark in Euclid by using its coordinates?

40. Use a map of your state to plan an airplane trip from your city or town to four other locations in your state. Write a set of directions for your trip that you could give to the pilot.

41. On grid paper, draw several parallelograms with diagonals that are perpendicular to each other. What do you observe about these parallelograms?

42. Find the areas of triangles *AST, BST, CST,* and *DST*. How do the areas compare? Why do you think this is true?

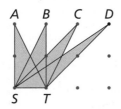

43. Find the areas of triangles *VMN, WMN, XMN, YMN,* and *ZMN*. How do the areas compare? Why do you think this is true?

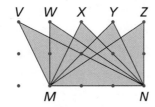

Mathematical Reflections

In this Investigation, you solved problems involving coordinate grids. You located points, calculated distances and areas, and found the vertices of polygons that satisfied given conditions. The following questions will help you summarize what you have learned.

Think about these questions. Discuss your ideas with other students and your teacher. Then write a summary of your findings in your notebook.

1. In the city of Euclid, **how** does the driving distance from one place to another compare to the flying distance?

2. Suppose you know the coordinates of two landmarks in Euclid. **How** can you find the distance between the landmarks?

3. **What** are some strategies for finding areas of figures drawn on a grid?

Common Core Mathematical Practices

As you worked on the Problems in this Investigation, you used prior knowledge to make sense of them. You also applied Mathematical Practices to solve the Problems. Think back over your work, the ways you thought about the Problems, and how you used Mathematical Practices.

Shawna described her thoughts in the following way:

We noticed that we could use a ruler to find the horizontal, vertical, or helicopter distance on the grid in Problem 1.1. Since each block was 1 centimeter, a ruler gave us another way to measure distance instead of counting blocks.

We also noticed that the diagonal of a square block is longer than each block, so counting blocks does not work for helicopter distances.

Common Core Standards for Mathematical Practice
MP5 Use appropriate tools strategically.

 • What other Mathematical Practices can you identify in Shawna's reasoning?

• Describe a Mathematical Practice that you and your classmates used to solve a different Problem in this Investigation.

Squaring Off

In this Investigation, you will explore the relationship between the side lengths and areas of squares. You will then use that relationship to find the lengths of segments on dot grids.

2.1 Looking for Squares

You can draw squares with different areas by connecting the points on a 5 dot-by-5 dot grid. Two simple examples follow.

area = 1 square unit   area = 4 square units

- What is the area of the largest square on a 5 dot-by-5 dot grid? Smallest square?

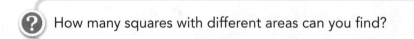

? How many squares with different areas can you find?

Common Core State Standards

8.NS.A.2 Use rational approximations of irrational numbers to compare the size of irrational numbers, locate them approximately on a number line diagram . . .

8.EE.A.2 Use square root and cube root symbols to represent solutions to equations of the form $x^2 = p$ and $x^3 = p$, where p is a positive rational number. Evaluate square roots of small perfect squares and cube roots of small perfect cubes . . .

Also N-Q.A.3

Problem **2.1**

A On 5 dot-by-5 dot grids, draw squares of various sizes by connecting dots. Draw squares with as many different areas as possible. Label each square with its area. Include at least two squares whose sides are not horizontal and vertical.

B Organize your set of squares by size. Then, describe the side lengths you found.

A)**C**)**E** Homework starts on page 29.

2.2 Square Roots

The area of a square is the length of a side multiplied by itself. This can be expressed by the formula $A = s \cdot s$, or $A = s^2$.

If you know the area of a square, you can work backward to find the length of a side. For example, suppose a square has an area of 4 square units. To find the length of a side, you need to figure out what positive number multiplied by itself equals 4. Because $2 \cdot 2 = 4$, the side length is 2 units. The number 2 is called a **square root** of 4.

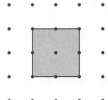

This square has an area of 4 square units. The length of each side is the square root of 4 units, which is equal to 2 units.

In general, if $A = s^2$, then s is a square root of A. Because $2 \cdot 2 = 4$ and $-2 \cdot (-2) = 4$, 2 and -2 are both square roots of 4. Every positive number has two square roots. The number 0 has only one square root, 0.

For any positive number N, $\sqrt{N}$ indicates the positive square root of N. For example, $\sqrt{4} = 2$. The negative square root of 4 is $-\sqrt{4} = -2$.

- What is the side length of a square with an area of 2 square units?

- Is this length greater than 1? Is it greater than 2?

- Is 1.5 a good estimate for $\sqrt{2}$?

- Can you find a better estimate for $\sqrt{2}$?

Problem 2.2

In this Problem, use your calculator only when instructed to do so.

A 1. Find the side lengths of squares with areas of 1, 9, 16, and 25 square units.

2. Find the values of $\sqrt{1}$, $\sqrt{9}$, $\sqrt{16}$, and $\sqrt{25}$.

B 1. What is the area of a square with a side length of 12 units? What is the area of a square with a side length of 2.5 units?

2. Find the missing numbers.

    a. $\sqrt{\blacksquare} = 12$ **b.** $\sqrt{\blacksquare} = 2.5$

3. Find x.

    a. $x^2 = 121$ **b.** $x^2 = 2.25$

    c. $\sqrt{x} = 121$ **d.** $\sqrt{2.25} = x$

4. Explain what each positive value of x in part (3) might represent in terms of area and length.

C Refer to the square with an area of 2 square units you drew in Problem 2.1. The exact side length of this square is $\sqrt{2}$ units.

1. Estimate $\sqrt{2}$ by measuring a side of the square with a centimeter ruler.

2. Calculate the area of the square, using your measurement from part (1). Is the result exactly equal to 2? Could you use your ruler to make a more accurate measurement for $\sqrt{2}$? Explain.

3. Use the square root key on your calculator to estimate $\sqrt{2}$.

4. How does your ruler estimate compare to your calculator estimate?

5. Suppose you are designing a square sand box that has an area of 2 square meters. What is a reasonable and accurate measure for the side length?

Problem 2.2 *continued*

D 1. Between which two consecutive whole numbers does $\sqrt{5}$ lie? Explain.

2. Which whole number from part (1) is closer to $\sqrt{5}$? Explain.

3. Without using your calculator, estimate the value of $\sqrt{5}$ to one decimal place.

4. Without using your calculator, can you get an even closer estimate than in part (3)?

E Give the exact side length of each square you drew in Problem 2.1.

ACE Homework starts on page 29.

2.3 Using Squares to Find Lengths

You can use a square to find the length of a segment connecting dots on a grid. For example, to find the length of the segment on the left, draw a square with the segment as a side. The square has an area of 5 square units, so the segment has an exact length of $\sqrt{5}$ units.

• How can you find the exact length of a line segment connecting any two dots on grid paper?

• How many different length segments can you draw on the 5 dot-by-5 dot grid?

Problem **2.3**

A **1.** On 5 dot-by-5 dot grids, draw line segments with as many different lengths as possible by connecting dots. Label each segment with its length. Use the $\sqrt{}$ symbol to express lengths that are not whole numbers. (**Hint:** You will need to draw squares that extend beyond the 5 dot-by-5 dot grids.)

2. List the lengths in increasing order.

3. Estimate each nonwhole number length to one decimal place. Then locate the lengths on a number line. How can you use the number line to decide which length is the greatest? Least?

4. Describe a situation where measuring to one decimal place is not accurate enough.

B **1.** Ella says the length of the segment in Figure 1 is $\sqrt{8}$ units. Oskar says it is $2\sqrt{2}$ units. Are both students correct? Explain.

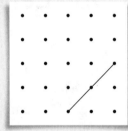

Figure 1

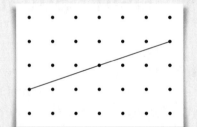

Figure 2

2. Express the exact length of the segment in Figure 2 in two ways.

3. Can you find a segment whose length cannot be expressed in two ways? Explain.

4. Which of the following lengths can be expressed in two ways: $\sqrt{5}$, $\sqrt{10}$, $\sqrt{18}$? Check your answers on a grid.

 Homework starts on page 29.

2.4 Cube Roots

The volume of a cube is the length of an *edge* multiplied by itself three times. Multiplying two edges of the base of a cube gives the area of the base. The area of the base times an edge that is the height gives the volume. The volume can be expressed by the formula $V = e \cdot e \cdot e$, or $V = e^3$.

If you know the volume of a cube, you can work backward to find the length of an edge. For example, suppose a cube has a volume of 8 cubic units. To find the length of an edge, you need to figure out what number multiplied by itself three times equals 8. Because $2 \cdot 2 \cdot 2 = 8$, the edge length is 2 units. The number 2 is called the **cube root** of 8.

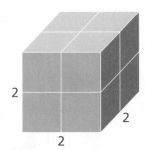

This cube has the volume of 8 cubic units. The length of each edge is the cube root of 8 units, which is equal to 2 units.

In general, if $V = e^3$, then e is the cube root of V. Because $2 \cdot 2 \cdot 2 = 8$, 2 is the cube root of 8. Because $-2 \cdot (-2) \cdot (-2) = -8$, -2 is the cube root of -8.

You can use the symbol, $\sqrt[3]{}$, to indicate cube root. For any number N, $\sqrt[3]{N}$ indicates the cube root of N. For example, $\sqrt[3]{8} = 2$ and $\sqrt[3]{-8} = -2$.

- How is finding the cube roots the same or different from finding square roots?

Problem 2.4

In this Problem, use your calculator only when instructed to do so.

A 1. Find the edge lengths of cubes with volumes of 1, 27, 64, and 125 cubic units.

    2. Find the values of $\sqrt[3]{1}$, $\sqrt[3]{27}$, $\sqrt[3]{64}$, and $\sqrt[3]{125}$.

B 1. What is the volume of a cube with an edge length of 5 units? What is the volume of a cube with an edge length of 2.5 units?

    2. Find the missing numbers.

      a. $\sqrt[3]{\blacksquare} = 5$ **b.** $\sqrt[3]{\blacksquare} = 2.5$

    3. Find x.

      a. $x^3 = 27$ **b.** $x^3 = -27$ **c.** $x^3 = \frac{1}{8}$

      d. $\sqrt[3]{x} = 27$ **e.** $\sqrt[3]{x} = -27$ **f.** $\sqrt[3]{x} = -\frac{1}{8}$

    4. Explain what each positive value of x might represent in terms of volume and length.

C 1. Between which two consecutive whole numbers does $\sqrt[3]{10}$ lie? Explain.

    2. Which whole number from part (1) is closer to $\sqrt[3]{10}$? Explain.

    3. Without using your calculator, estimate the value of $\sqrt[3]{10}$ to one decimal place.

    4. Without using your calculator, can you get an even closer estimate than in part (3)?

    5. Three students find the edge length for a cube with a volume of 10 cubic feet. How might have each student arrived at their answer?

      Nick: 2.15 feet   Josie: 2.1 feet   Kevin: 2.1544 feet

D 1. Which is greater, $\sqrt{8}$ or $\sqrt[3]{8}$?

    2. Which is greater, $\sqrt{N}$ or $\sqrt[3]{N}$? Explain.

ACE Homework starts on page 29.

Applications

1. Find the area of every square that can be drawn by connecting dots on a 3 dot-by-3 dot grid.

2. On dot paper, draw a hexagon with an area of 16 square units.

3. On dot paper, draw a square with an area of 2 square units. Write an argument to convince a friend that the area is 2 square units.

For Exercises 4–37, do not use the $\sqrt{}$ key on your calculator.

4. Graph the following set of numbers in order on a number line.

2.3	$2\frac{1}{4}$	$\sqrt{5}$	$\sqrt{2}$	$\frac{5}{2}$	$\sqrt{4}$
4	-2.3	$-2\frac{1}{4}$	$\frac{4}{2}$	$-\frac{4}{2}$	2.09

For Exercises 5–7, estimate each square root to one decimal place.

5. $\sqrt{11}$

6. $\sqrt{30}$

7. $\sqrt{172}$

8. **Multiple Choice** Between which pair of numbers does $\sqrt{15}$ lie?

   A. 3.7 and 3.8

   B. 3.8 and 3.9

   C. 3.9 and 4.0

   D. 14 and 16

Find exact values for each square root.

9. $\sqrt{144}$

10. $\sqrt{0.36}$

11. $\sqrt{961}$

Find the two consecutive whole numbers between which each square lies. Explain.

12. $\sqrt{27}$

13. $\sqrt{1,000}$

Tell whether each statement is true.

14. $6 = \sqrt{36}$ **15.** $1.5 = \sqrt{2.25}$ **16.** $11 = \sqrt{101}$

Find the missing number.

17. $\sqrt{\blacksquare} = 81$ **18.** $14 = \sqrt{\blacksquare}$ **19.** $\blacksquare = \sqrt{28.09}$

20. $\sqrt{\blacksquare} = 3.2$ **21.** $\sqrt{\blacksquare} = \frac{1}{4}$ **22.** $\sqrt{\frac{4}{9}} = \blacksquare$

Find each product.

23. $\sqrt{2} \cdot \sqrt{2}$ **24.** $\sqrt{3} \cdot \sqrt{3}$

25. $\sqrt{4} \cdot \sqrt{4}$ **26.** $\sqrt{5} \cdot \sqrt{5}$

Find the positive and negative square roots of each number.

27. 1 **28.** 4 **29.** 2

30. 16 **31.** 25 **32.** 5

Find x.

33. $x^2 = 144$ **34.** $x^2 = \frac{1}{4}$ **35.** $\sqrt{x} = \frac{1}{4}$ **36.** $\sqrt{\frac{1}{4}} = x$ **37.** $\sqrt{144} = x$

38. Consider segment AB at the right.

  a. On dot paper, draw a square with side AB. What is the area of the square?

  b. Use a calculator to estimate the length of segment AB.

39. Consider segment CD at the right.

  a. On dot paper, draw a square with side CD. What is the area of the square?

  b. Use a calculator to estimate the length of segment CD.

40. Find the area and the side length of this square.

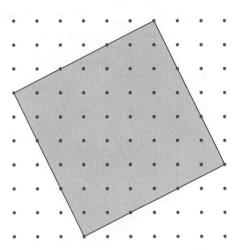

41. Find the length of every line segment that can be drawn by connecting dots on a 3 dot-by-3 dot grid.

42. Consider this segment.

    a. Express the length of the segment, using the $\sqrt{}$ symbol.

    b. Between which two consecutive whole numbers does the length of the segment lie?

43. Show that $2\sqrt{5}$ is equal to $\sqrt{20}$ by finding the length of line segment AC in two ways.

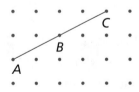

44. Multiple Choice Which line segment has a length of $\sqrt{17}$ units?

F.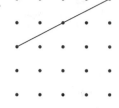

G.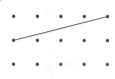

H.

J.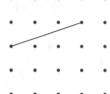

For Exercise 45 and 46, find the length of each side of the figure.

45.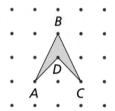

46.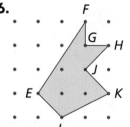

Find the edge length of a cube with the given volume.

47. 216 cube units   **48.** 512 cubic inches   **49.** 1,000 cubic feet

Find the value of each cube root.

50. $\sqrt[3]{216}$ **51.** $\sqrt[3]{512}$ **52.** $\sqrt[3]{1,000}$

Find the volume of a cube with the given edge length.

53. 6 yards   **54.** 8 inches   **55.** 10 feet

Find the missing number.

56. $\sqrt[3]{\blacksquare} = 6$ **57.** $\sqrt[3]{\blacksquare} = 8$ **58.** $\sqrt[3]{\blacksquare} = 10$

59. a. Between which two consecutive whole numbers does $\sqrt[3]{80}$ lie? Explain.

   b. Which whole number from part (a) is closer to $\sqrt[3]{80}$? Explain.

   c. Estimate the value of $\sqrt[3]{80}$ to one decimal place.

Find x.

   60. $x^3 = 64$ **61.** $x^3 = -64$ **62.** $x^3 = \frac{27}{64}$ **63.** $\sqrt[3]{x} = -8$ **64.** $\sqrt[3]{-8} = x$

Connections

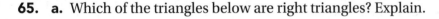

65. a. Which of the triangles below are right triangles? Explain.

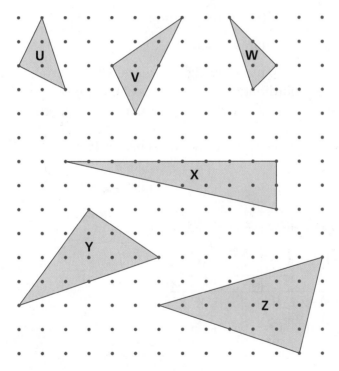

   b. Find the area of each right triangle.

66. Refer to the squares you drew in Problem 2.1.

   a. Find the perimeter of each square to the nearest hundredth of a unit.

   b. What rule can you use to calculate the perimeter of a square when you know the length of a side?

67. In Problem 2.1, it was easier to find the "upright" squares. Two of these squares are represented on the coordinate grid.

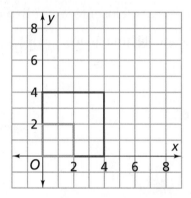

a. Are these squares similar? Explain.

b. How are the coordinates of the corresponding vertices related?

c. How are the areas of the squares related?

d. Copy the drawing. Add two more "upright" squares with a vertex at (0, 0). How are the coordinates of the vertices of these new squares related to the 2 × 2 square? How are their areas related?

68. On grid paper, draw coordinate axes like the ones below. Plot point P at $(1, -2)$.

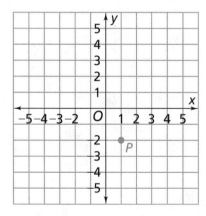

a. Draw a square $PQRS$ with an area of 10 square units.

b. Name a vertex of your square that is $\sqrt{10}$ units from point P.

c. Give the coordinates of at least two other points that are $\sqrt{10}$ units from point P.

69. In Problem 2.3, you drew segments of length 1 unit, $\sqrt{2}$ units, 4 units, and so on. On a copy of the number line below, locate and label each length you drew. On the number line, $\sqrt{1}$ and $\sqrt{2}$ have been marked as examples.

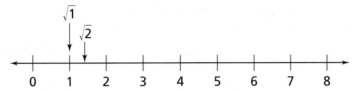

70. Sketch a cube with a volume of 64 cube units. Label the edge length of the cube on your drawing.

Extensions

71. On dot paper, draw a nonrectangular parallelogram with an area of 6 square units.

72. On dot paper, draw a triangle with an area of 5 square units.

73. Dalida claims that $\sqrt{8} + \sqrt{8}$ is equal to $\sqrt{16}$ because 8 plus 8 is 16. Is she right? Explain.

You know that $\sqrt{5} \cdot \sqrt{5} = \sqrt{5 \cdot 5} = \sqrt{25} = 5$. Tell whether each product is a whole number. Explain.

74. $\sqrt{2} \cdot \sqrt{50}$ **75.** $\sqrt{4} \cdot \sqrt{16}$ **76.** $\sqrt{4} \cdot \sqrt{6}$

77. The drawing shows three right triangles with a common side.

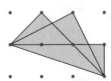

    a. Find the length of the common side.

    b. Do the three triangles have the same area? Explain.

You know that $\sqrt[3]{4} \cdot \sqrt[3]{4} \cdot \sqrt[3]{4} = \sqrt[3]{4 \cdot 4 \cdot 4} = \sqrt[3]{64} = 4$. Tell whether each product is a whole number. Explain.

78. $\sqrt[3]{5} \cdot \sqrt[3]{25}$ **79.** $\sqrt[3]{4} \cdot \sqrt[3]{16}$ **80.** $\sqrt[3]{5} \cdot \sqrt[3]{125}$

In this Investigation, you worked with square roots and cube roots, and explored squares and segments drawn on dot paper. You learned that the side length of a square is the positive square root of the square's area. You also discovered that, in many cases, a square root is not a whole number. The following questions will help you summarize what you have learned.

Think about these questions. Discuss your ideas with other students and your teacher. Then write a summary of your findings in your notebook.

1. **Describe** how you would find the length of a line segment connecting two dots on dot paper. Be sure to consider horizontal, vertical, and tilted segments.

2. a. **Explain** what it means to find the square root of a number.

   b. **Explain** whether or not a number can have more than one square root.

3. a. **Explain** what it means to find the cube root of a number.

   b. **Explain** whether or not a number can have more than one cube root.

Common Core Mathematical Practices

As you worked on the Problems in this Investigation, you used prior knowledge to make sense of them. You also applied Mathematical Practices to solve the Problems. Think back over your work, the ways you thought about the Problems, and how you used Mathematical Practices.

Ken described his thoughts in the following way:

In Problem 2.1, we showed that we had a square using the same reasoning we used in Problem 1.2 to show that the figures we drew on the coordinate grid were squares, rectangles, and right triangles. Then, to find the area of the square, we counted the number of square units inside the square.

Common Core Standards for Mathematical Practice

MP8 Look for and express regularity in repeated reasoning.

- What other Mathematical Practices can you identify in Ken's reasoning?

- Describe a Mathematical Practice that you and your classmates used to solve a different Problem in this Investigation.

The Pythagorean Theorem

In earlier grades, you learned about the properties of triangles. In this Investigation, you will learn about a special property of one type of triangle.

- What are characteristics that all triangles share?

- In what ways are the three triangles below different?

- How do the three side lengths of any triangle relate to each other?

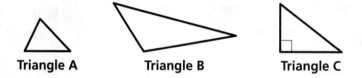

Triangle A   Triangle B   Triangle C

Triangle A is an acute triangle. An **acute triangle** has three acute angles.

Triangle B is an obtuse triangle. An **obtuse triangle** has one obtuse angle.

Triangle C is a right triangle. A **right triangle** has one angle with a measure of exactly 90°. A 90° angle is called a *right angle* and is often marked with a small square. The longest side of a right triangle is the side opposite the right angle. This side is called the **hypotenuse.** The other two sides are called the **legs.**

- Can a triangle have more than one angle that is 90°? Explain.

....

Common Core State Standards

8.G.B.6 Explain a proof of the Pythagorean Theorem and its converse.

8.G.B.7 Apply the Pythagorean Theorem to determine unknown side lengths in right triangles in real-world and mathematical problems in two and three dimensions.

8.G.B.8 Apply the Pythagorean Theorem to find the distance between two points in a coordinate system.

3.1 Discovering the Pythagorean Theorem

In this Investigation, you will use squares to find the side lengths of the acute, right, and obtuse triangles shown below.

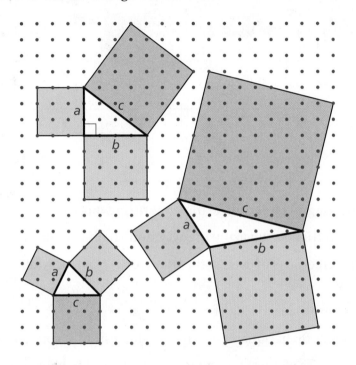

- Is there a relationship among the areas of squares drawn on the sides of a triangle?
- If so, what is the relationship?
- Is this relationship the same for all types of triangles?

Problem 3.1

A **1.** Make a copy of the table below. Record the areas and lengths for the three given triangles.

Type of Triangle	Area of Square on Side a	Area of Square on Side b	Area of Square on Side c	Length of Side a	Length of Side b	Length of Side c
Right	■	■	■	■	■	■
Right	■	■	■	■	■	■
Acute	■	■	■	■	■	■
Acute	■	■	■	■	■	■
Obtuse	■	■	■	■	■	■
Obtuse	■	■	■	■	■	■

2. On dot paper or grid paper, make three more drawings.

- Draw a right triangle, an acute triangle, and an obtuse triangle.

- Label the three sides of each of the triangles a, b, and c, where c the longest side.

- Draw a square on each side of the triangles.

- Find the areas of the squares and record the results in your table.

- Find the lengths of the sides and record the results in your table.

B **1.** For each triangle, look for a relationship among the areas of the three squares on the sides. Make a conjecture about the areas of the squares drawn on the sides of a triangle and the type of triangle.

2. Test your conjecture by drawing another triangle.

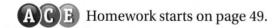 Homework starts on page 49.

3.2 A Proof of the Pythagorean Theorem

The pattern you discovered in Problem 3.1 is a theorem in mathematics. A **theorem** is a general mathematical statement that has been proven true. This theorem is named after the Greek mathematician Pythagoras. The **Pythagorean Theorem** states a relationship among the lengths of the sides of a right triangle. It is one of the most famous theorems in mathematics.

More than 300 different proofs have been given for the Pythagorean Theorem. One of these proofs is based on the geometric argument you will explore in this Problem.

Did You Know?

Pythagoras lived in the 500s B.C. He had a devoted group of followers known as the Pythagoreans.

The Pythagoreans were a powerful group. Their influence became so strong that some people feared they threatened the local political structure. They were forced to disband. However, many Pythagoreans continued to meet in secret and to teach the ideas of Pythagoras.

I had help!

PYTHAGORAS

The Pythagoreans held Pythagoras in high regard—so high that they gave him credit for all of their discoveries. Much of what we now attribute to Pythagoras may actually be the work of one or several of his followers. That includes the Pythagorean Theorem.

You can use the puzzle pieces below to explore the Pythagorean Theorem.

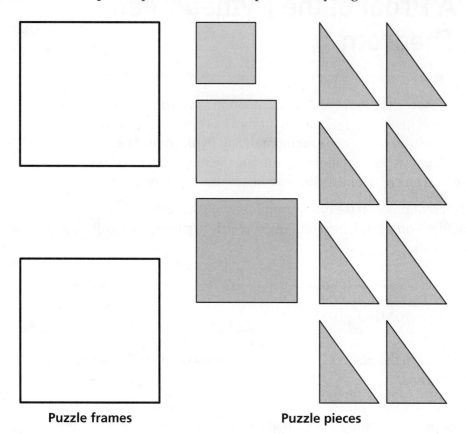

Puzzle frames   **Puzzle pieces**

? How can you use these puzzle pieces to prove the Pythagorean Theorem geometrically?

Problem 3.2

Copy the shapes on the previous page or use the puzzle pieces your teacher gives you.

A Study a triangle piece and the three square puzzle pieces. How do the side lengths of the squares compare to the side lengths of the triangle?

B 1. Arrange the 11 puzzle pieces to fit exactly into the two puzzle frames.

 2. What conclusion can you draw about the relationship among the areas of the three colored squares?

 3. What does the conclusion you reached in part (2) mean in terms of the side lengths of the triangles?

 4. Compare your results with those of another group. Did that group come to the same conclusion your group did? Is this conclusion true for all right triangles? Explain.

C Suppose a right triangle has legs of length 3 centimeters and 5 centimeters.

 1. Use your conclusion from Question B to find the area of a square drawn on the hypotenuse of the triangle.

 2. What is the length of the hypotenuse?

D In Problem 3.1 and Problem 3.2, you have explored the Pythagorean Theorem, a relationship among the side lengths of a right triangle. State this theorem as a rule for any right triangle with leg lengths a and b and hypotenuse length c.

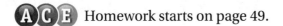 **A C E** Homework starts on page 49.

3.3 Finding Distances

In Investigation 2, you found the lengths of tilted segments by drawing squares and finding their areas. You can also find these lengths using the Pythagorean Theorem.

- • How can you use the Pythagorean Theorem to find the distance between any two points on a dot grid?

- • How can you use it to find the end points of a line with length $\sqrt{13}$ units?

Problem 3.3

In Questions A–D, refer to the grid below.

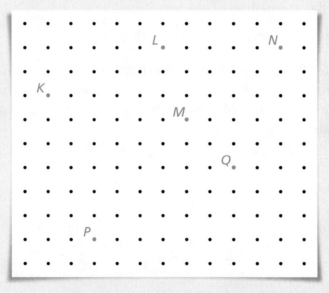

A 1. Copy the points above onto dot paper. Then, draw a right triangle with segment *KL* as its hypotenuse.

2. Find the lengths of the legs of the triangle.

3. Use the Pythagorean Theorem to find the length of segment *KL*.

Problem **3.3** | *continued*

B Find the distance between points *M* and *N* by connecting them with a segment and using the method in Question A.

C Find the distance between points *P* and *Q*.

D In Problem 1.1, Question C, you found the driving distance between the stadium at (−2, 3) and the high school at (1, 8). What is the helicopter distance between these two locations? Estimate the difference of the two distances.

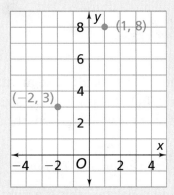

E Find the coordinates of two points that are $\sqrt{13}$ units apart. Label the points *R* and *S*. Explain how you know the distance between the points is $\sqrt{13}$ units.

A C E Homework starts on page 49.

3.4 Measuring the Egyptian Way
Lengths That Form a Right Triangle

 In ancient Egypt, the Nile River overflowed every year. It flooded the surrounding lands and often removed markers for property boundaries. As a result, the Egyptians had to remeasure their land every year.

Because many plots of land were rectangular, the Egyptians needed a reliable way to mark right angles. They devised a clever method involving a rope with equally spaced knots that formed 12 equal intervals.

To understand the Egyptians' method, mark off 12 segments of the same length on a piece of rope or string. Tape the ends of the string together to form a closed loop. Form a right triangle with side lengths that are whole numbers of segments.

- What are the side lengths of the triangle you formed?
- What are some ways you could check that this is a right triangle?
- How do you think the Egyptians used the knotted rope?

In this Problem, you will explore these questions about the opposite, or *converse*, of the Pythagorean Theorem:

- Is any triangle whose side lengths *a, b,* and *c* satisfy the relationship $a^2 + b^2 = c^2$ a right triangle?

- Suppose the side lengths of a triangle do not satisfy the relationship $a^2 + b^2 = c^2$. Does this mean the triangle is *not* a right triangle?

Problem **3.4**

A Copy the table below. Each row gives three side lengths. Use string, straws, or polystrips to build triangles with the given side lengths. Then, complete the second and third columns of the table.

Side Lengths (units)	Do the side lengths satisfy $a^2 + b^2 = c^2$?	Is the triangle a right triangle?
3, 4, 5	▪	▪
5, 12, 13	▪	▪
5, 6, 10	▪	▪
6, 8, 10	▪	▪
4, 4, 4	▪	▪
1, 2, 2	▪	▪

B 1. Make a conjecture about triangles with side lengths that satisfy the relationship $a^2 + b^2 = c^2$.

2. Make a conjecture about triangles with side lengths that do *not* satisfy the relationship $a^2 + b^2 = c^2$.

3. Check your conjecture with two other triangles.

continued on the next page >

Problem **3.4** *continued*

C Determine whether a triangle with the given side lengths is a right triangle.

1. 12 units, 16 units, 20 units

2. 8 units, 15 units, 17 units

3. 12 units, 9 units, 16 units

4. Diego says he knew that one of the above triangles would be a right triangle. It is a scale copy of one of the right triangles in Question A. Do you agree with his thinking? Explain.

5. Raeka claims that if the lengths of three sides of a triangle satisfy the relationship $a^2 + b^2 = c^2$, then the triangle is a right triangle. She reasons as follows:

- Take the two shorter side lengths a and b. Use these to form a right angle and then a right triangle. Call the length of the hypotenuse d.

- Since this triangle is a right triangle, then $a^2 + b^2 = d^2$.

- You also know that $a^2 + b^2 = c^2$. Therefore, $c^2 = d^2$, or $c = d$.

- Since three sides of one triangle are the same as the three sides of another triangle, then these two triangles are the same. This means that the original right triangle is unique.

Does Raeka's reasoning prove the conjecture that if $a^2 + b^2 = c^2$, then the triangle with side lengths a, b, and c is a right triangle? Explain.

D The Egyptians' knotted rope had 12 segments. The rope could be used to make several triangles with whole-number side lengths. Only one of the combinations of side lengths gives a right triangle.

1. What combination of whole-number side lengths makes a right triangle? How do you know this combination makes a right triangle?

2. What combination of whole-number side lengths makes a nonright triangle? How do you know this combination is not a right triangle?

A C E Homework starts on page 49.

 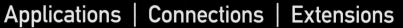

Applications

1. The diagram below shows a right triangle with a square on each side.

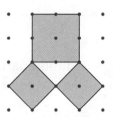

   a. Find the areas of the three squares.

   b. Use the areas from part (a) to show that the squares on the sides of this triangle satisfy the Pythagorean relationship, $a^2 + b^2 = c^2$.

2. The triangle below is a right triangle. Show that this triangle satisfies the Pythagorean Theorem.

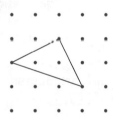

3. A right triangle has legs of length 5 inches and 12 inches.

   a. Find the area of a square drawn on the hypotenuse of the triangle.

   b. Find the length of the hypotenuse.

4. Use the Pythagorean Theorem to find the length of the hypotenuse of this triangle.

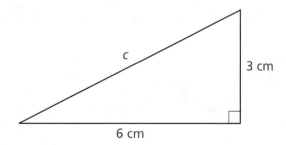

In Exercises 5 and 6, find each missing length.

5.

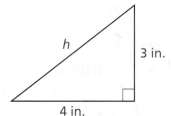

6.

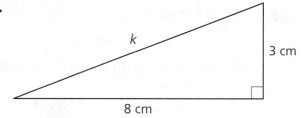

7. On dot paper, find two points that are $\sqrt{17}$ units apart. Label the points W and X. Explain how you know the distance between the points is $\sqrt{17}$ units.

8. On dot paper, find two points that are $\sqrt{20}$ units apart. Label the points Y and Z. Explain how you know the distance between the points is $\sqrt{20}$ units.

For Exercises 9–12, use the map of Euclid. Find the flying distance in blocks between each pair of landmarks without using a ruler. Explain.

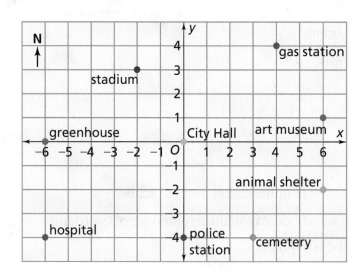

9. greenhouse and stadium

10. police station and art museum

11. greenhouse and hospital

12. City Hall and gas station

13. **Multiple Choice** Refer to the map of Euclid. Which landmarks are $\sqrt{40}$ blocks apart?

   A. greenhouse and stadium

   B. City Hall and gas station

   C. hospital and art museum

   D. animal shelter and police station

14. **Multiple Choice** Which set of side lengths makes a right triangle?

   F. 10 cm, 24 cm, 26 cm

   G. 4 cm, 6 cm, 10 cm

   H. 5 cm, 10 cm, $\sqrt{50}$ cm

   J. 8 cm, 9 cm, 15 cm

In Exercises 15 and 16, tell whether the triangle with the given side lengths is a right triangle.

15. 10 cm, 10 cm, $\sqrt{200}$ cm

16. 9 in., 16 in., 25 in.

Connections

17. The prism below has a base that is a right triangle.

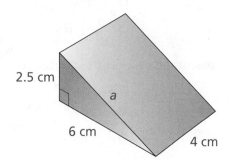

2.5 cm

6 cm

a

4 cm

   a. What is the value of a?

   b. Do you need to know the value of a to find the volume of the prism? Do you need to know the value of a to find the surface area? Explain.

   c. What is the volume?

   d. What is the surface area?

   e. Sketch a net for the prism.

For Exercises 18–21, refer to the figures below.

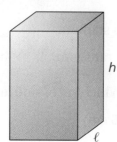
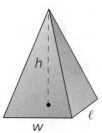

Cylinder   Cone   Prism   Pyramid

18. **Multiple Choice** Which expression represents the volume of the cylinder?

    A. $2\pi r^2 + 2\pi rh$ **B.** $\pi r^2 h$

    C. $\frac{1}{3}\pi r^2 h$ **D.** $\frac{1}{2}\pi r^2 h$

19. **Multiple Choice** Which expression represents the volume of the cone?

    F. $2\pi r^2 + 2\pi rh$ **G.** $\pi r^2 h$

    H. $\frac{1}{3}\pi r^2 h$ **J.** $\frac{1}{2}\pi r^2 h$

20. **Multiple Choice** Which expression represents the volume of the prism?

    A. $2(\ell w + \ell h + wh)$ **B.** ℓwh

    C. $\frac{1}{3}\ell wh$ **D.** $\frac{1}{2}\ell wh$

21. **Multiple Choice** Which expression represents the volume of the pyramid?

    F. $2(\ell w + \ell h + wh)$ **G.** ℓwh

    H. $\frac{1}{3}\ell wh$ **J.** $\frac{1}{2}\ell wh$

22. Nayo draws a quadrilateral. It has adjacent sides measuring 16 inches and 20 inches and a diagonal measuring 25 inches. Is her quadrilateral a rectangle? Explain.

23. Bo is building a tree house. He has marked locations for four holes that will hold his corner posts. They form a figure with a long side of 12 feet and a short side of 9 feet. What must the diagonal of the figure be to make sure the base of his tree house is a rectangle?

24. One method for checking whether a wall is perpendicular to the ground involves a 10-foot pole. A builder makes a mark exactly 6 feet high on the wall, and rests one end of the pole at that mark. The other end of the pole rests on the ground. A triangle is formed.

If the triangle is a right triangle, how far from the base of the wall is the bottom of the pole? Explain.

25. In the city of Euclid, Hilary's house is located at $(5, -3)$, and Jamilla's house is located at $(2, -4)$.

a. Without plotting points, find the shortest driving distance in blocks between the two houses.

b. What is the exact flying distance between the two houses?

26. Which labeled point is the same distance from point *A* as point *B* is from point *A*? Explain.

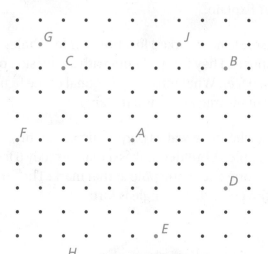

Extensions

27. Find the missing lengths.

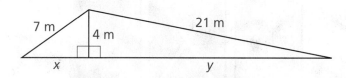

28. Jolon looks at the diagram below. He says, "If the center of this circle is at the origin, then I can figure out the radius."

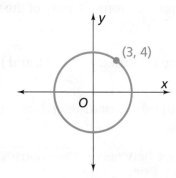

a. Explain how Jolon can find the radius.

b. What is the radius?

In Exercises 29–31, you will look for relationships among the areas of shapes other than squares drawn on the sides of a right triangle.

29. Half circles have been drawn on the sides of this right triangle.

   a. Find the area of each half circle.

   b. How are the areas of the half circles related?

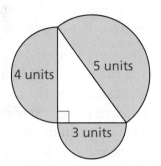

30. Equilateral triangles have been drawn on the sides of this right triangle.

   a. Find the area of each equilateral triangle.

   b. How are the areas of the equilateral triangles related?

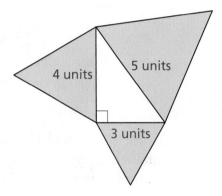

31. Regular hexagons have been drawn on the sides of this right triangle.

   a. Find the area of each hexagon.

   b. How are the areas of the hexagons related?

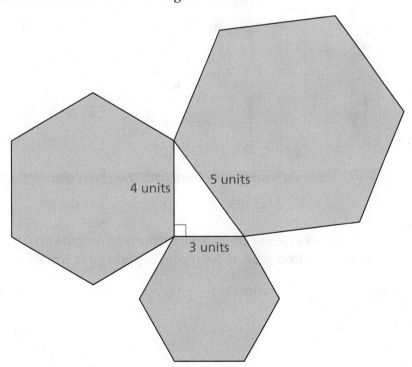

32. Any tilted segment that connects two dots on dot paper can be the hypotenuse of a right triangle. You can use this idea to draw segments of a given length. The key is finding two square numbers with a sum equal to the square of the length you want to draw.

For example, suppose you want to draw a segment with length $\sqrt{5}$ units. You can draw a right triangle in which the sum of the areas of the squares on the legs is 5. The area of the square on the hypotenuse will be 5 square units, so the length of the hypotenuse will be $\sqrt{5}$ units. Because 1 and 4 are square numbers, and $1 + 4 = 5$, a right triangle with legs of lengths 1 unit and 2 units has a hypotenuse of length $\sqrt{5}$ units.

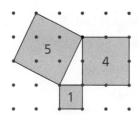

a. To use this method, it helps to be familiar with sums of square numbers. Copy and complete the addition table to show the sums of pairs of square numbers.

+	1	4	9	16	25	36	49	64
1	2	5						
4	5							
9								
16								
25								
36								
49								
64								

For parts (b)–(d), find two square numbers with the given sum.

b. 10   **c.** 25   **d.** 89

For parts (e)–(h), draw tilted segments with the given lengths on dot paper. Use the addition table to help you. Explain your work.

e. $\sqrt{26}$ units   **f.** 10 units   **g.** $\sqrt{10}$ units   **h.** $\sqrt{50}$ units

For Exercises 33–38, tell whether it is possible to draw a segment of the given length by connecting dots on dot paper. Explain.

33. $\sqrt{2}$ units

34. $\sqrt{3}$ units

35. $\sqrt{4}$ units

36. $\sqrt{5}$ units

37. $\sqrt{6}$ units

38. $\sqrt{7}$ units

39. Use the graph to answer parts (a)–(c).

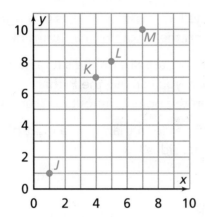

   a. Find the coordinates of points J and K.

   b. Use the coordinates to find the distance from point J to point K. Explain your method.

   c. Use your method from part (b) to find the distance from point L to point M.

Mathematical Reflections 3

In this Investigation, you worked with a very important mathematical relationship called the Pythagorean Theorem. The following questions will help you summarize what you have learned.

Think about these questions. Discuss your ideas with other students and your teacher. Then write a summary of your findings in your notebook.

1. Suppose you are given the lengths of two sides of a right triangle. **Describe** how you can find the length of the third side.

2. Suppose two points on a grid are not on the same horizontal or vertical line. **Describe** how you can use the Pythagorean Theorem to find the distance between the points without measuring.

3. **How** can you determine whether a triangle is a right triangle if you know only the lengths of its sides?

Common Core Mathematical Practices

As you worked on the Problems in this Investigation, you used prior knowledge to make sense of them. You also applied Mathematical Practices to solve the Problems. Think back over your work, the ways you thought about the Problems, and how you used Mathematical Practices.

Hector described his thoughts in the following way:

In Problem 3.1, we found a rule about the areas of the squares on the sides of a right triangle. We noticed in Problem 3.4 that we could apply our rule to triangles with side lengths that were a multiple of the lengths of our original triangle.

We knew that a triangle with sides measuring 3, 4, and 5 was a right triangle. So a triangle with sides measuring 6, 8, and 10 would also be a right triangle because the triangles are similar. We did not have to check it with our theorem.

....

Common Core Standards for Mathematical Practice

MP8 Look for and express regularity in repeated reasoning.

• What other Mathematical Practices can you identify in Hector's reasoning?

• Describe a Mathematical Practice that you and your classmates used to solve a different Problem in this Investigation.

Using the Pythagorean Theorem: Understanding Real Numbers

In Investigation 3, you studied the Pythagorean Theorem.

The area of the square on the hypotenuse of a right triangle is equal to the sum of the areas of the squares on the legs.

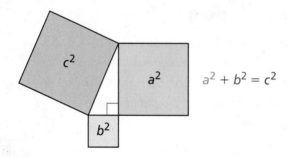

$$a^2 + b^2 = c^2$$

In this Investigation, you will explore some interesting applications of the Pythagorean Theorem.

. . . .

Common Core State Standards

8.NS.A.1 Understand informally that every number has a decimal expansion; the rational numbers are those with decimal expansions that terminate in 0s or eventually repeat. Know that other numbers are called irrational.

8.NS.A.2 Use rational approximations of irrational numbers to compare the size of irrational numbers, locate them approximately on a number line diagram, and estimate the value of expressions (e.g., π^2).

8.G.B.7 Apply the Pythagorean Theorem to determine unknown side lengths in right triangles in real-world and mathematical problems in two and three dimensions.

Also 8.EE.A.2, 8.EE.C.7a, A-CED.A.1, N-Q.A.3

4.1 Analyzing the Wheel of Theodorus
Square Roots on a Number Line

The diagram below is named for its creator, Theodorus of Cyrene (sy ree nee), a former Greek colony. Theodorus was a Pythagorean.

The Wheel of Theodorus begins with a triangle with legs 1 unit long and winds around counterclockwise. Each triangle is drawn using the hypotenuse of the previous triangle as one leg and a segment of length 1 unit as the other leg. To make the Wheel of Theodorus, you need only know how to draw right angles and segments 1 unit long.

The Wheel of Theodorus

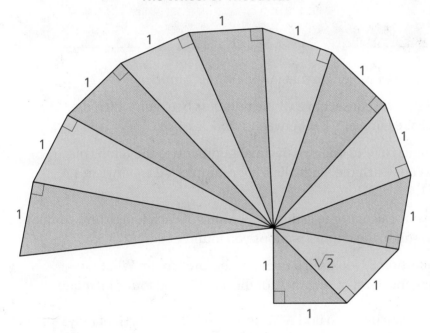

- What are the lengths of the spokes of the wheel?

Problem 4.1

A Use the Pythagorean Theorem to find the length of each hypotenuse in the Wheel of Theodorus. On a copy of the wheel, label each hypotenuse with its length. Use the $\sqrt{\ }$ symbol to express lengths that are not whole numbers.

B Use a cut-out copy of the ruler below to measure each hypotenuse on the wheel. Label the place on the ruler that represents the length of each hypotenuse. For example, the first hypotenuse length would be marked like this:

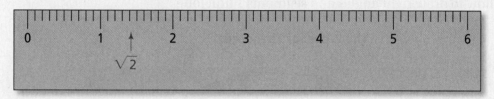

C For each hypotenuse length that is not a whole number:

1. Give the two consecutive whole numbers between which the length lies. For example, $\sqrt{2}$ is between 1 and 2.

2. Use your ruler to find two decimal numbers (to the tenths place) between which the length lies. For example, $\sqrt{2}$ is between 1.4 and 1.5.

3. Use your calculator to estimate the value of each length and compare the result to the approximations you found in part (2).

4. In Question B, you used a ruler to measure length. What is a reasonable level of accuracy for the lengths you found? Explain.

D Joey uses his calculator to find $\sqrt{3}$. He gets 1.732050808. Geeta says this must be wrong because when she multiplies 1.732050808 by 1.732050808, she gets 3.000000001. Why do these students disagree?

A C E Homework starts on page 71.

4.2 Representing Fractions as Decimals

Rational numbers are numbers that you can express as ratios of integers. For example, $\frac{3}{4}$, $\frac{-2}{5}$, $\frac{5}{7}$, $\frac{7}{3}$, $\frac{4}{1}$ (or 4), and $-2\frac{1}{2}$ $\left(\text{or } -\frac{5}{2}\right)$ are rational numbers.

You can also represent rational numbers as decimals. In your earlier math work, you learned that you can express as a decimal any fraction with a numerator and a denominator that are integers. You find the decimal by dividing the numerator by the denominator.

In the examples below, you can see that sometimes the decimal representation terminates after a limited number of digits. These decimals are **terminating decimals.** Sometimes the decimal representation has a repeating pattern of digits that never ends. These decimals are **repeating decimals.**

$$\frac{5}{16} = 0.3125$$
$$\frac{-7}{3} = -7 \div 3 = -2.333333\ldots$$
$$-1\frac{3}{7} = \frac{-10}{7} = -1.428571428571\ldots$$

You can write a repeating decimal with a bar over the repeating digits: $-1.\overline{428571}$.

However, there are other decimal numbers that neither terminate nor repeat. Here are two examples of decimal numbers that have a pattern, but do not terminate or repeat a set of digits.

$$1.010010001000010000010000000\ldots$$
$$10.11121314151617181920212223242526272 8\ldots$$

• What would be the next four digits in each string of digits?

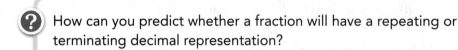

You have seen rational numbers, such as $\frac{1}{3}$, with decimal representations that are repeating decimals. You have also seen rational numbers, such as $\frac{5}{16}$, with decimal representations that are terminating decimals.

- Is the decimal representation for any rational number always a repeating or terminating decimal; or can you represent some rational numbers as nonterminating, nonrepeating decimals?

(?) How can you predict whether a fraction will have a repeating or terminating decimal representation?

Problem 4.2

Ⓐ Use a calculator to write each fraction as a decimal. Tell whether the decimal is *terminating* or *repeating*. If the decimal is repeating, tell which digits repeat.

1. $\frac{2}{5}$ 2. $\frac{1}{4}$ 3. $\frac{3}{8}$ 4. $\frac{1}{16}$

5. $\frac{35}{10}$ 6. $\frac{2}{3}$ 7. $\frac{8}{99}$ 8. $\frac{170}{999}$

Ⓑ 1. Jose says he knows that the decimal representation of a fraction, such as $\frac{3}{8}$, will be a terminating decimal if he can scale up the denominator to make a power of 10. What scale factor would Jose need to use to rewrite $\frac{3}{8}$ as $\frac{x}{1,000}$? What is the decimal representation?

2. Mei says she can scale up $\frac{2}{3}$ to $\frac{66\frac{2}{3}}{100}$, but the decimal representation of $\frac{2}{3}$ is a repeating decimal. Do Jose and Mei disagree? Explain.

3. Make a conjecture about how to predict when a fraction will have a terminating decimal representation. Test your conjecture on the following fractions:

     $\frac{4}{7}$ $\frac{5}{6}$ $\frac{25}{12}$ $\frac{19}{20}$

Problem 4.2 *continued*

C For each decimal, find three equivalent fractions, if possible.

1. 0.3

2. 0.3333 . . .

3. 0.13133133313333 . . .

D **1.** Nic's calculator batteries are dead so he has to do the long division to find a decimal representation for $\frac{2}{7}$.

$$
\begin{array}{r}
0.285 \\
7\overline{)2.000} \\
-14 \\
\hline
60 \\
-56 \\
\hline
40 \\
-35 \\
\hline
5
\end{array}
$$

Continue the long division process until you are sure you can predict whether this decimal is terminating, repeating, or neither. Explain why you think your prediction is correct. Then, check your answer on a calculator.

2. Is it possible for a fraction to have a decimal equivalent that does *not* repeat and does *not* terminate? Explain.

A C E Homework starts on page 71.

4.3 Representing Decimals as Fractions

In Problem 4.2, you found that you can represent every rational number in fraction form as a terminating or repeating decimal. In this Problem, you will investigate how to do the reverse and represent decimals as fractions.

- Can you represent every repeating or terminating decimal as a fraction?

Problem 4.3

A **1.** On a copy of the table below, write each fraction as a decimal.

Fraction	Decimal	Fraction	Decimal
$\frac{1}{9}$	▪	$\frac{1}{11}$	▪
$\frac{2}{9}$	▪	$\frac{2}{11}$	▪
$\frac{3}{9}$	▪	$\frac{3}{11}$	▪
$\frac{4}{9}$	▪	$\frac{4}{11}$	▪
$\frac{5}{9}$	▪	$\frac{5}{11}$	▪
$\frac{6}{9}$	▪	$\frac{6}{11}$	▪
$\frac{7}{9}$	▪	$\frac{7}{11}$	▪

2. Describe any patterns you see in your table.

B Use the patterns you found in Question A to write a decimal representation for each rational number. Use your calculator to check your work.

1. $\frac{9}{9}$ **2.** $-\frac{10}{9}$ **3.** $\frac{10}{11}$ **4.** $\frac{^-12}{11}$

Problem **4.3** continued

C Find a fraction equivalent to each decimal, if possible.

1. $1.222\ldots$ **2.** $2.777\ldots$ **3.** $0.818181\ldots$

4. $0.27277277727777\ldots$ **5.** 1.99999 **6.** $0.99999\ldots$

D The patterns from Question A can help you represent some repeating decimals as fractions. What about other repeating decimals, such as $0.121212\ldots$? You need a method that will help you find an equivalent fraction for any repeating decimal.

1. Suppose $x = 0.121212\ldots$. What is $100x$? Is it still a repeating decimal?

2. Complete the subtraction.

$$
\begin{aligned}
100x &= 12.121212\ldots \\
- \quad x &= 0.121212\ldots \\
\hline
99x &= \blacksquare
\end{aligned}
$$

Is the answer for $99x$ still a repeating decimal?

3. Find a fraction form for $0.121212\ldots$ by solving for x.

4. Why do you think this method starts out by multiplying by 100? Explain.

5. Use this method to write each repeating decimal as a fraction.

a. $0.151515\ldots$ **b.** $0.123123123\ldots$ **c.** $1.354354354\ldots$

E Tell whether each statement is *true* or *false*.

1. You can write any fraction as a terminating or repeating decimal.

2. You can write any terminating or repeating decimal as a fraction.

ACE Homework starts on page 71.

4.4 Getting Real
Irrational Numbers

In Problem 4.2, you saw that 10.111213141516 . . . is an example of a decimal that never repeats and never terminates. Here is another example:

$$0.12122122212222 \ldots$$

- Why does this pattern go on forever without repeating?

You can never represent a nonrepeating, nonterminating decimal as a fraction, or rational number. For example, $\frac{1}{10}$ is a close fraction representation of the decimal above, $\frac{12}{100}$ is closer, and $\frac{121}{1,000}$ is even closer. You cannot, however, get an exact fraction representation for this decimal.

- How is this kind of decimal the same as or different from the repeating decimal 0.6666 . . . ? The repeating decimal 0.121212 . . . ? The terminating decimal 1.414213562?

Numbers with decimal representations that are nonterminating and nonrepeating are called **irrational numbers.** Some irrational numbers have patterns, as above. Some have no patterns, but the decimals never terminate and never repeat. You cannot express these numbers as ratios of integers.

You have worked with irrational numbers before. For example, the decimal representation of the number π starts with the digits 3.14159265 . . . and goes forever without repeating any sequence of digits. The number π is irrational.

The number $\sqrt{2}$ is also irrational. You could not find an exact terminating or repeating decimal representation for $\sqrt{2}$ because such a representation does not exist! Other irrational numbers are $\sqrt{3}$, $\sqrt{5}$, and $\sqrt{11}$. In fact, $\sqrt{n}$ is an irrational number for any whole number value of n that is not a square number.

- Are the following numbers rational or irrational: $\sqrt{7}$, $\sqrt{9}$, $\sqrt{0.25}$? Why or why not?

- Can you give another number that has a rational square root?

- Can you give another number that does not have a rational square root?

The set of irrational and rational numbers is called the set of **real numbers.** An amazing fact is that there are an infinite number of irrational numbers between any two fractions! You will explore irrational and rational numbers in this Problem.

Problem 4.4

A **1.** Write three or more nonterminating, nonrepeating decimals that are greater than 0.5 but less than 0.6.

 2. Why is there no limit to the number of nonterminating, nonrepeating decimals that are between 0.5 and 0.6?

B **1.** Write a rational-number estimate for $\sqrt{5}$ that is less than $\sqrt{5}$ and one that is greater than $\sqrt{5}$.

 2. Write an irrational-number estimate for $\sqrt{5}$ that is less than $\sqrt{5}$ and one that is greater than $\sqrt{5}$.

C **1.** The diagram shows a square drawn on the hypotenuse of a right triangle. Find the lengths of the sides of the square and the area of the square. If you use a ruler to measure the hypotenuse, how accurate can you be? Explain.

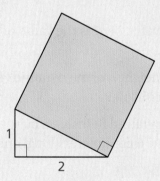

 2. Ty says that this proves that $\sqrt{5} \cdot \sqrt{5} = 5$. Do you agree? Explain.

continued on the next page >

Problem 4.4 *continued*

D Tell whether each number is *rational* or *irrational*. Explain your reasoning.

1. $\sqrt{7}$ 2. $\sqrt{16}$ 3. $\sqrt{4} \cdot \sqrt{4}$

4. $\sqrt{7} \cdot \sqrt{7}$ 5. $2\sqrt{7}$ 6. $\sqrt{28}$

7. $\sqrt{14}$ 8. $\sqrt{\frac{1}{16}}$ 9. 2.45455

10. 2.45454545...   11. 2.454554555...   12. 2.455455545555...

E As part of her math project, Angela is making a pyramid. She starts with the net shown below, drawn on centimeter grid paper.

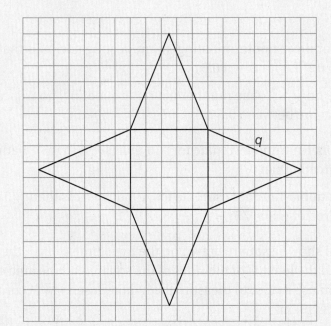
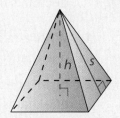

1. What is the exact value of *q*? Is the value of *q* a rational or irrational number? Explain.

2. What is the exact height *h* of the pyramid? Is the height a rational or irrational number? Explain.

3. Will the finished pyramid fit inside a cube-shaped box that is 6 centimeters wide, 6 centimeters long, and 6 centimeters high? Explain.

A C E Homework starts on page 71.

Applications | Connections | Extensions

Applications

1. The hypotenuse of a right triangle is 15 centimeters long. One leg is 9 centimeters long. How long is the other leg?

2. The Wheel of Theodorus in Problem 4.1 includes only the first 11 triangles in the wheel. The wheel can go on forever.

   a. Find the side lengths of the next three triangles.

   b. Find the areas of the first five triangles in the wheel. Describe any patterns you observe.

   c. Suppose you continue adding triangles to the wheel. Which triangle will have a hypotenuse of length 5 units?

Write each fraction as a decimal. Tell whether the decimal is *terminating* or *repeating*. If the decimal is repeating, tell which digits repeat.

3. $\frac{5}{8}$ 4. $\frac{3}{5}$ 5. $\frac{1}{6}$ 6. $\frac{4}{99}$ 7. $\frac{43}{10}$

Find a fraction equivalent to each terminating decimal.

8. 0.1875   9. 5.125   10. 43.6

11. a. Explore decimal representations of fractions with a denominator of 99. Look at fractions less than 1: $\frac{1}{99}$, $\frac{2}{99}$, $\frac{3}{99}$, and so on. What pattern do you see?

   b. Write a decimal representation for the fraction $\frac{51}{99}$.

12. a. Explore decimal representations of fractions with a denominator of 999. Look at fractions less than 1: $\frac{1}{999}$, $\frac{2}{999}$, $\frac{3}{999}$, and so on. What pattern do you see?

   b. Write a decimal representation for the fraction $\frac{1,000}{999}$.

Use the patterns you discovered in Problem 4.3 and Exercises 11 and 12 to find a fraction or mixed number equivalent to each decimal.

13. 0.3333 . . .

14. 0.050505 . . .

15. 0.454545 . . .

16. 0.045045 . . .

17. 10.121212 . . .

18. 3.9999 . . .

19. The decimal below is close to, but between, which two fractions? (**Hint:** There is more than one answer to this question.)

$$0.101001000100001 . . .$$

20. Find an irrational number between 6.23 and 6.35.

21. Find an irrational number between $\frac{1}{7}$ and $\frac{1}{6}$.

Find the length of diagonal *d* in each rectangular prism.

22.

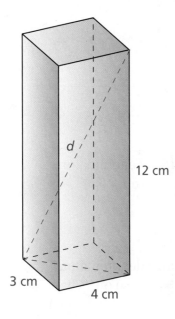

12 cm

3 cm

4 cm

23.

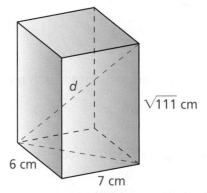

$\sqrt{111}$ cm

6 cm

7 cm

Connections

24. **Multiple Choice** Which set of irrational numbers is in order from least to greatest?

   A. $\sqrt{2}, \sqrt{5}, \sqrt{11}, \pi$

   B. $\sqrt{2}, \sqrt{5}, \pi, \sqrt{11}$

   C. $\sqrt{2}, \pi, \sqrt{5}, \sqrt{11}$

   D. $\pi, \sqrt{2}, \sqrt{5}, \sqrt{11}$

Find the two consecutive whole numbers the square root is between. Explain.

25. $\sqrt{39}$ 26. $\sqrt{600}$

Tell whether the statement is *true* or *false*. Explain.

27. $0.06 = \sqrt{0.36}$

28. $1.1 = \sqrt{1.21}$

29. $20 = \sqrt{40}$

Tell whether a triangle with the given side lengths is a right triangle. Explain how you know.

30. 5 cm, 7 cm, $\sqrt{74}$ cm

31. $\sqrt{2}$ ft, $\sqrt{3}$ ft, 3 ft

Estimate the square root to one decimal place *without* using the $\sqrt{}$ key on your calculator. Then, tell whether the number is *rational* or *irrational*.

32. $\sqrt{121}$ 33. $\sqrt{0.49}$

34. $\sqrt{15}$ 35. $\sqrt{1,000}$

36. In the drawing below, the cone and the cylinder have the same height and radius. Suppose the radius *r* of the cone is 2 units and the slant height *s* is $\sqrt{29}$ units.

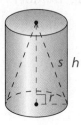

    a. What is the height of the cone?

    b. What is the volume of the cone?

37. In the drawing below, the pyramid and the cube have the same height and base.

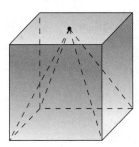

    a. Suppose the edge length of the cube is 6 units. What is the volume of the pyramid?

    b. Suppose the edge length of the cube is *x* units. What is the volume of the pyramid?

Extensions

Find the area of the shaded region.

38.

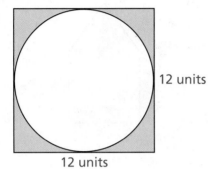

12 units

12 units

39.

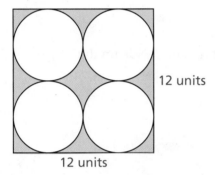

12 units

12 units

40.

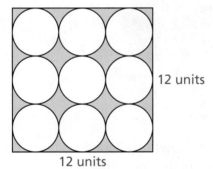

12 units

12 units

41. Simplify each expression. Leave your answer as either an integer or a square root.

  a. $\sqrt{2} \cdot 2\sqrt{2}$ **b.** $2 \div \sqrt{2}$ **c.** $\sqrt{2}\,(1 + \sqrt{2}) - \sqrt{2}$

42. Below are a square pyramid and its net.

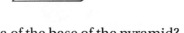

  a. What is the area of the base of the pyramid?

  b. What is the surface area of the pyramid?

  c. What is the height of the pyramid?

  d. What is the volume of the pyramid?

43. The managers of Izzie's Ice Cream Shop are trying to decide on the best size for their waffle cones.

  a. Izzie suggests that the cone should have a diameter of 4.5 inches and a height of 6 inches. What is the volume of the cone that Izzie suggests?

  b. Izzie's sister, Becky, suggests that the cone should have a height of 6 inches and a slant height of 7 inches. (The slant height is labeled s in the diagram.) What is the volume of the cone that Becky suggests?

In this Investigation, you looked at decimal representations of fractions and fraction representations of decimals. You discovered that some decimals do not terminate or repeat. You cannot represent these decimals as fractions with numerators and denominators that are integers. The following questions will help you summarize what you have learned.

Think about these questions. Discuss your ideas with other students and your teacher. Then write a summary of your findings in your notebook.

1. **Give** three examples of fractions with decimal representations that terminate.

2. **Give** three examples of fractions with decimal representations that repeat.

3. **Give** three examples of irrational numbers, including one irrational number greater than 5.

4. **How** can you determine whether you can write a given decimal as a fraction?

Common Core Mathematical Practices

As you worked on the Problems in this Investigation, you used prior knowledge to make sense of them. You also applied Mathematical Practices to solve the Problems. Think back over your work, the ways you thought about the Problems, and how you used Mathematical Practices.

Elena described her thoughts in the following way:

In Problem 4.3, we noticed a pattern among certain fractions that had 9's in the denominators. We found a specific group of fractions that we could represent as repeating decimals. We made a conjecture based on this pattern that we could represent fractions of the form $\frac{n}{9}$ by the decimal $0.nnnn\ldots$, where n is a positive whole number. Then we used our conjecture to find the decimal representations of other fractions that followed this same pattern.

Common Core Standards for Mathematical Practice
MP7 Look for and make use of structure.

- What other Mathematical Practices can you identify in Elena's reasoning?

- Describe a Mathematical Practice that you and your classmates used to solve a different Problem in this Investigation.

Investigation 5

Using the Pythagorean Theorem: Analyzing Triangles and Circles

In this Investigation, you will apply the Pythagorean Theorem in some very different situations. Whenever there is a right triangle in a figure, you can use the Pythagorean Theorem to deduce the side lengths of the triangle. Sometimes the triangle is not obvious.

5.1 Stopping Sneaky Sally
Finding Unknown Side Lengths

A baseball diamond is actually a square. If you can find right triangles in this shape, you can use the Pythagorean Theorem to solve problems about distances.

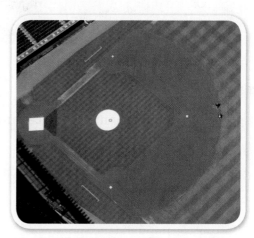

Common Core State Standards

8.G.A.4 Understand that a two-dimensional figure is similar to another if the second can be obtained from the first by a sequence of rotations, reflections, translations, and dilations; given two similar two-dimensional figures, describe a sequence that exhibits the similarity between them.

8.G.B.7 Apply the Pythagorean Theorem to determine unknown side lengths in right triangles in real-world and mathematical problems in two and three dimensions.

8.G.B.8 Apply the Pythagorean Theorem to find the distance between two points in a coordinate system.

Also A-CED.A.2, A-REI.D.10, N-Q.A.3

Problem 5.1

Horace Hanson is the catcher for the Humboldt Bees baseball team. Sneaky Sally Smith, the star of the Canfield Cats, is on first base. Sally is known for stealing bases, so Horace is keeping an eye on her.

The pitcher throws a fastball, and the batter swings and misses. Horace catches the pitch and, out of the corner of his eye, he sees Sally take off for second base.

Use the diagram to answer Questions A–C.

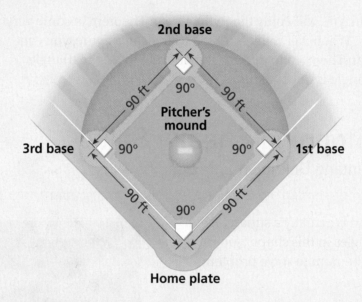

A **1.** How far must Horace throw the baseball to get Sally out at second base? Explain.

2. Jen says the distance that Horace throws the baseball is a rational number. Funda says that it is an irrational number. Explain each student's reasoning.

B The shortstop is standing on the baseline, halfway between second base and third base. How far is the shortstop from Horace?

C The pitcher's mound is 60 feet 6 inches from home plate. Use this information and your answer to Question A to find the distance from the pitcher's mound to each base.

A C E Homework starts on page 88.

Did You Know?

Most people consider baseball an American invention. A similar game called *rounders*, however, was played in England as early as the 1600s. Like baseball, rounders involved hitting a ball and running around bases. However, in rounders, the fielders actually threw the ball at the base runners. If a ball hit a runner while he was off base, he was out.

Alexander Cartwright was a founding member of the Knickerbockers Base Ball Club of New York City, baseball's first organized club. Cartwright played a key role in writing the first set of formal rules for baseball in 1845.

According to Cartwright's rules, a batter was out if a fielder caught the ball either on the fly or on the first bounce. Today, balls caught on the first bounce are not outs. Cartwright's rules also stated that the first team to have 21 runs at the end of an inning was the winner. Today, the team with the highest score after nine innings wins the game.

5.2 Analyzing Triangles

You can use the Pythagorean Theorem to investigate some interesting properties of an equilateral triangle. One property is that all equilateral triangles have reflection symmetries.

Triangle *ABC* is an equilateral triangle. Line *AP* is a reflection line for triangle *ABC*. If you fold an equilateral triangle along the line of reflection, you will find some properties of any equilateral triangle.

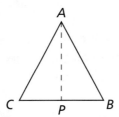

- What is true about the angle measures of an equilateral triangle?

- What is true about the side lengths of an equilateral triangle?

- What can you say about the measures of angle *CAP*, angle *BAP*, angle *CPA*, and angle *BPA*?

- What can you say about line segments *CP* and *BP*?

- What can you say about triangles *ACP* and *ABP*?

- Is there a relationship among the lengths of line segments *CP*, *AP*, and *AC*?

Problem 5.2

Ⓐ Suppose the lengths of the sides of equilateral triangle *ABC* above are 2 units. On a copy of triangle *ABC*, label the following measures:

1. angle *CAP*   **2.** angle *BAP*

3. angle *CPA*   **4.** angle *BPA*

5. length of *CP*   **6.** length of *BP*

7. length of *AP*

Problem 5.2 *continued*

B Suppose the lengths of the sides of equilateral triangle *ABC* on the facing page are 4 units. On a copy of triangle *ABC*, label the following measures:

1. angle *CAP*   **2.** angle *BAP*

3. angle *CPA*   **4.** angle *BPA*

5. length of *CP*   **6.** length of *BP*

7. length of *AP*

C Thang thinks he has a way of predicting the length of the height *AP* for any equilateral triangle. He has drawn the results of Questions A and B in the diagram below.

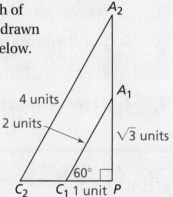

1. The triangles look similar. Are they? Explain.

2. What is the length of A_2P? What is the length of C_2P?

3. Is the length of A_2P the same as the length of *AP* you found in Question B? Explain.

D A right triangle with a 60° angle is called a 30-60-90 triangle. The 30-60-90 triangle at the right has a hypotenuse of length 10 units.

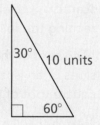

1. What are the lengths of the other two sides? Explain how you found your answers.

2. What relationships among the side lengths do you observe for this 30-60-90 triangle? Is this relationship true for all 30-60-90 triangles? Explain.

3. If the hypotenuse of a 30-60-90 triangle is *s* units long, what are the lengths of the other two sides?

continued on the next page >

Problem 5.2 *continued*

E Use the figure below.

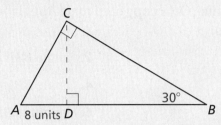

C

30°

A 8 units D B

1. How many right triangles do you see in the figure?

2. Find the perimeter of triangle *ABC*. Explain your strategy.

3. Find the area of triangle *ABC*. Explain your strategy.

A C E Homework starts on page 88.

Did You Know?

In the movie *The Wizard of Oz*, the scarecrow celebrates his new brain by reciting the following:

"The sum of the square roots of any two sides of an isosceles triangle is equal to the square root of the remaining side."

Now you know what the scarecrow meant to say, even though his still imperfect brain got it wrong.

Given an isosceles triangle, suppose the sides with equal lengths are *s* units and the base is *b* units. Then one possible way to represent what the scarecrow said is:

$$\sqrt{s} + \sqrt{s} = \sqrt{b}$$

• Can you think of two numbers that would make this statement true?

• Could the numbers you thought of be the lengths of the sides of an isosceles triangle?

5.3 Analyzing Circles

A Cartesian coordinate plane can be helpful for the study of geometric figures because you can locate and label points on the figure using coordinates. A circle with its center at the origin is shown below. The **radius** of a circle is the distance from the center to any point on the circle.

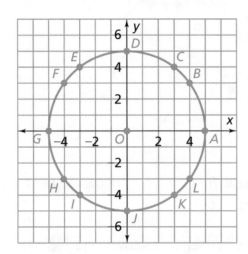

- How can you use the Pythagorean Theorem to find radius *OC*? Radius *OB*? Radius *OL*? Explain.

- What is the radius of the circle above?

> ? If the coordinates of a point on a circle centered at the origin is (*x*, *y*), what is the relationship between *x* and *y*?

Problem 5.3

Ⓐ Dustin looks at the diagram below. He says, "If the center of this circle is at the origin, then I can find the length of the radius."

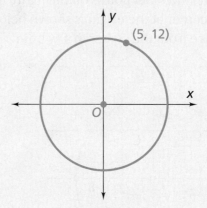

1. Explain how Dustin can find the length of the radius of this circle.

2. What is the length of the radius?

Ⓑ The coordinates of a point on the circle below are (x, y).

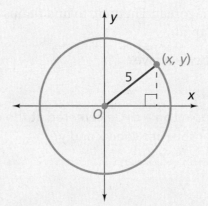

1. Use the Pythagorean Theorem to write an equation showing a relationship between x and y.

2. Would your equation describe the relationship between coordinates (x, y) for any point on any circle? Explain.

Problem **5.3** | *continued*

C   **1.** Use the Pythagorean Theorem to write the equation of any circle with a center at the origin and radius r.

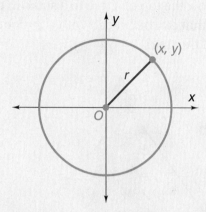

2. The hospital in a big city is located at $(0, 0)$ on a gridded map. The lines on the grid are 1 mile apart. The paramedics make a circle on a map, showing all the locations within a helicopter distance of 10 miles of the hospital. Which equation matches the circle they draw? Explain.

    I. $x^2 + y^2 = 10$

    II. $x^2 + y^2 = 20$

    III. $x^2 + y^2 = 100$

3. A stadium is 5 miles east and 5 miles north of the hospital. It is located at $(5, 5)$ on the map. Is this inside, outside, or on the circle drawn by the paramedics?

 Homework starts on page 88.

Applications

1. At an evergreen farm, the taller trees are braced by wires. A wire extends from 2 feet below the top of a tree to a stake in the ground. What is the tallest tree that can be braced with a 25-foot wire staked 15 feet from the base of the tree?

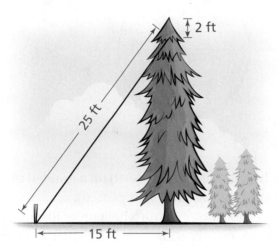

2. Scott, a college student, needs to walk from his dorm room in Wilson Hall to his math class in Wells Hall. Normally, he walks 500 meters east and 600 meters north along the sidewalks, but today he is running late. He decides to take the shortcut through the Quad.

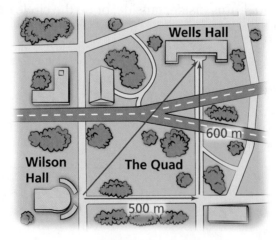

   a. How many meters long is Scott's shortcut?

   b. How much shorter is the shortcut than Scott's usual route?

3. Sierra wants to buy a new laptop computer. She likes two computers that look very similar. Sierra wants to figure out how they differ. Here are her two options:

  Option 1: 13-inch screen with a 5.5-inch side length

  Option 2: 13.3-inch screen with a 5.1-inch side length

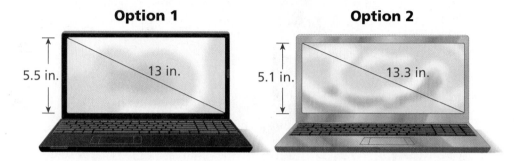

Option 1   **Option 2**

5.5 in.   13 in.   5.1 in.   13.3 in.

  a. What are the dimensions of the rectangular computer screen for each option?

  b. Which screen has the greater area?

4. Kala and Ali are making a kite. To make the frame, they place a 40-inch stick horizontally across a 60-inch stick so that both sides of the horizontal stick are equal in length. Then they tie the two sticks together with the string to form right angles. The longer part of the 60-inch stick measures 50 inches, as shown below.

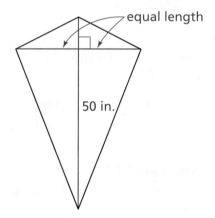

equal length

50 in.

Kala says that 130 inches of string will be enough to stretch all around the kite frame. Ali says that they will need at least 153 inches of string. Who is correct? Explain.

5. As part of his math assignment, Santos has to estimate the height of a lighthouse. He decides to use what he knows about 30-60-90 triangles. Santos makes the measurements shown below. About how tall is the tower? Explain.

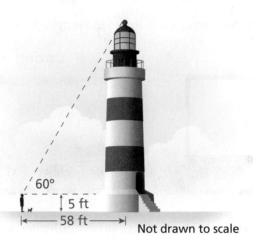

60°

5 ft

58 ft

Not drawn to scale

6. Use the figure below.

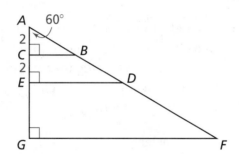

A   60°
2
C
2
E
B
D
G
F

a. Name all the 30-60-90 triangles in the figure. Are all of these triangles similar to each other? Explain.

b. Find the ratio of the length of segment BA to the length of segment AC. What can you say about the corresponding ratio in the other 30-60-90 triangles?

c. Find the ratio of the length of segment BC to the length of segment AC. What can you say about the corresponding ratios in the other 30-60-90 triangles?

d. Find the ratio of the length of segment BC to the length of segment AB. What can you say about the corresponding ratios in the other 30-60-90 triangles?

e. Suppose segment AG is 8 units long. How long are segments AF and GF?

7. Use the figure below.

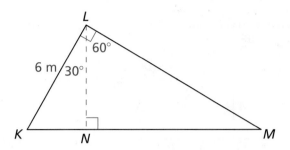

a. How many 30-60-90 triangles do you see in the figure?

b. What is the perimeter of triangle *KLM*?

8. In Problem 5.2, you found the side lengths of the triangle below left.

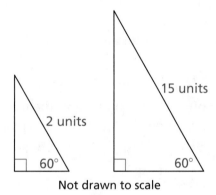

Not drawn to scale

a. Explain how you know that the triangle on the right is similar to the triangle on the left.

b. Use the side lengths of the smaller triangle to find the unknown side lengths of the larger triangle. Explain.

c. How are the areas of the two triangles related?

9. Use the circle below.

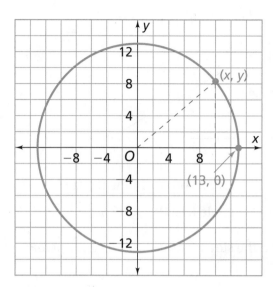

a. Write an equation that relates x and y for any point (x, y) on the circle.

b. Find the missing coordinates for each of these points on the circle. If there is more than one possible point, give the missing coordinate for each possibility. Show that each ordered pair satisfies the equation.

$(0, \blacksquare)$ $\qquad$ $(5, \blacksquare)$ $\qquad$ $(-4, \blacksquare)$ $\qquad$ $(-8, \blacksquare)$

$(\blacksquare, 10)$ $\qquad$ $(\blacksquare, -6)$ $\qquad$ $(\blacksquare, 0)$ $\qquad$ $(\blacksquare, -2)$

10. Use the circle below.

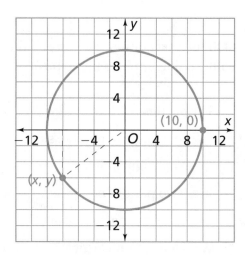

a. Write an equation that relates x and y for any point (x, y) on the circle.

b. Find the missing coordinates for each of these points on the circle. If there is more than one possible point, give the missing coordinate for each possibility. Show that each ordered pair satisfies the equation.

$(8, \blacksquare)$ $(3, \blacksquare)$ $(-4, \blacksquare)$ $(0, \blacksquare)$

$(\blacksquare, -4)$ $(\blacksquare, -6)$ $(\blacksquare, 0)$ $(\blacksquare, 2)$

11. Jada's parents get a new wireless router that has signal range up to 1,400 feet. Jada wants to know whether she will have Internet access in her tree house. She makes a coordinate map of their house with the router at the origin.

a. Jada's tree house is located at $(600, 800)$ on her coordinate map. Will Jada have an Internet connection? Explain.

b. What is the equation of the circle representing Internet coverage?

Connections

12. For each type of quadrilateral in the first column, identify all the properties from the second column that apply to that type of quadrilateral.

Quadrilateral Types

a. square

b. rectangle

c. rhombus

d. parallelogram

Properties

i. Two pairs of parallel sides

ii. Four right angles

iii. Two pairs of congruent sides

iv. Interior angle measures with a sum of 360°

v. Opposite angle measures with a sum of 180°

vi. Perpendicular diagonals

13. A tangram is a puzzle that contains seven pieces: 5 isosceles right triangles, a parallelogram, and a square. You can form a big square by putting all seven pieces together. Suppose the length of the leg of the small isosceles right triangle is 1.7 centimeters. What is the side length of the big square? (**Hint:** Two small triangles can form the medium-sized right triangle and the parallelogram.)

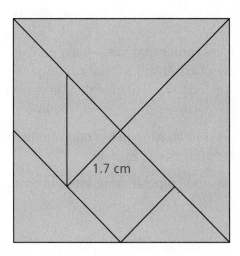

1.7 cm

Two cars leave a city at noon. One car travels north and the other travels east. Use this information for Exercises 14 and 15.

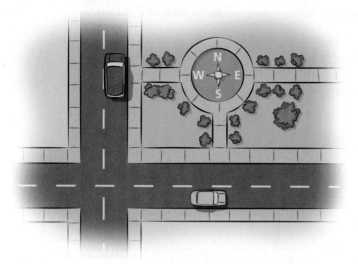

14. Suppose the northbound car is traveling at 60 miles per hour and the eastbound car is traveling at 50 miles per hour. Make a table that shows the distance each car has traveled and the distance between the two cars after 1 hour, 2 hours, 3 hours, and so on. Describe how the distances are changing.

15. Suppose the northbound car is traveling at 40 miles per hour. After 2 hours, the cars are 100 miles apart. How fast is the other car going? Explain.

16. Square *ABCD* has sides of length 1 unit. Copy the square. Draw diagonal *BD*, forming two triangles. Cut out the square and fold it along the diagonal.

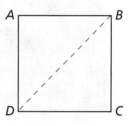

   a. How do the two triangles compare?

   b. Find the angle measures for one of the triangles. Explain how you found each measure.

   c. What is the length of the diagonal? Explain.

   d. Suppose square *ABCD* had sides of length 5 units instead of 1 unit. How would this change your answers to parts (b) and (c)?

17. A right triangle with a 45° angle is called a 45-45-90 triangle, or an isosceles right triangle.

    a. Are all 45-45-90 triangles similar to each other? Explain.

    b. Suppose one leg of a 45-45-90 triangle is 5 units long. Find the perimeter of the triangle.

18. The diagram shows tram cars gliding along a cable. How long is the cable to the nearest tenth of a meter?

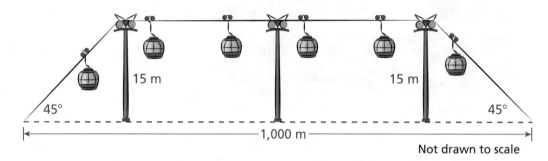

15 m   15 m

45°   45°

1,000 m

Not drawn to scale

19. Ming is building a large equilateral triangle using pattern blocks that are small equilateral triangles. Each side of the triangular pattern blocks measures $1\frac{1}{2}$ inches.

    a. Ming thinks that four pattern blocks will be enough to make the large equilateral triangle. Do you agree with him? Use a drawing to explain.

    b. What is the height of the large equilateral triangle?

    c. Pat claims that he can transform this large equilateral triangle into a rectangle if he can use pattern blocks that are cut in half. Is this possible? If so, what are the dimensions of this rectangle?

For Exercises 20–31, find the value of each expression.

20. $12 + (-18)$ **21.** $-9 + (-19)$ **22.** $-32 - 73$

23. $-23 - (-12)$ **24.** $90 - (-24)$ **25.** $34 - 76$

26. $-23 \cdot (-3)$ **27.** $5 \cdot (-13)$ **28.** $-12 \cdot 20$

29. $-24 \div 6$ **30.** $-42 \div (-2)$ **31.** $84 \div (-4)$

Write an equation for the line with the given slope and y-intercept.

32. slope $\frac{1}{2}$, y-intercept $(0, 3)$

33. slope $-\frac{1}{3}$, y-intercept $(0, 5)$

34. slope 6, y-intercept $(0, \frac{1}{2})$

Write an equation for the line with the given slope and that passes through the given point.

35. slope 2, point $(3, 1)$

36. slope -4, point $(-1, 7)$

37. slope $-\frac{5}{6}$, point $(0, 5)$

38. In the design below, the radius of the circle is 6 meters.

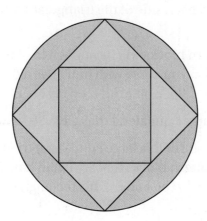

a. What is the side length of the larger square? What is the area of the larger square?

b. What is the area of the smaller square?

c. What is the area of the region between the smaller and larger squares?

d. What is the area of the region between the larger square and the circle?

39. Use the design below.

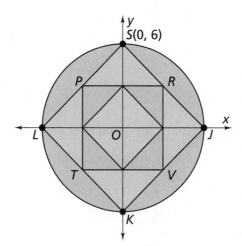

a. Find the equation of the circle.

b. Find the length of segment *LS* and the area of square *LSJK*.

c. Find the length of segment *PR* and the area of square *PRVT*.

d. What are the coordinates of points *P* and *R*? Explain.

Extensions

40. The roads connecting a store, a library, and a movie theater form a right triangle. It takes half an hour to go from the store to the library traveling at 50 miles per hour. It takes half an hour to go from the library to the movie theater traveling at 60 miles per hour.

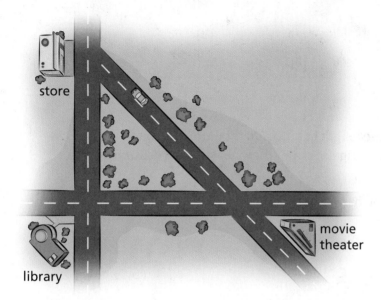

   a. How far is it from the store to the movie theater?

   b. How long will it take to travel from the store to the movie theater traveling at 55 miles per hour?

41. Segment *AB* below makes a 45° angle with the *x*-axis. The length of segment *AB* is 5 units.

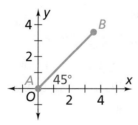

   a. Find the coordinates of point *B* to two decimal places.

   b. What is the slope of line *AB*?

42. In origami, you mostly use square paper. However, if you want to make a flower with three petals, you need to use paper in the shape of an equilateral triangle. You can make paper in the shape of an equilateral triangle from square paper.

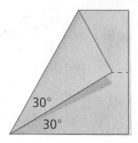
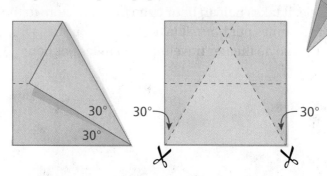

a. What is the side length of an equilateral triangle made out of a piece of square origami paper that measures 15 centimeters by 15 centimeters?

b. What is the height of the equilateral triangle?

43. Use the figure below.

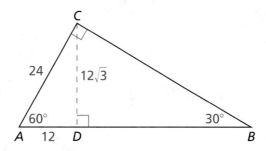

a. What is the length of segment *BD*? Segment *AB*?

b. What is the length of segment *BC*?

c. Ky figures the area of triangle *ABC* is $\frac{1}{2}(24)(24\sqrt{3})$ square units. Is he correct? Explain his reasoning.

d. Mario thinks the area of triangle *ABC* is $\frac{1}{2}(48)(12\sqrt{3})$ square units. Is he correct? Explain his reasoning.

e. Jen thinks the area of triangle *ABC* is $\frac{1}{2}(12)(12\sqrt{3}) + \frac{1}{2}(36)(12\sqrt{3})$ square units. Is she correct? Explain her reasoning.

f. Are the answers in parts (c)–(e) equivalent? Explain.

44. Use the design below.

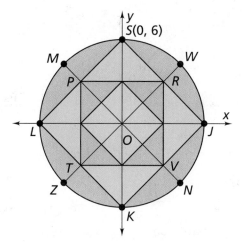

a. What are the coordinates of points *P*, *R*, *V*, and *T*?

b. What is the equation of the line through points *R* and *T*?

c. If you extend the line through points *R* and *T*, the line would meet the circle at two points, *W* and *Z*. What are the coordinates of points *W* and *Z*? Explain how you know these points are on the circle.

d. If you extend the line through points *P* and *V*, the line would meet the circle at two points, *M* and *N*. What are the coordinates of points *M* and *N*?

e. Is *WMZN* a square? Explain.

45. This circle has radius 5 and center (1, 2).

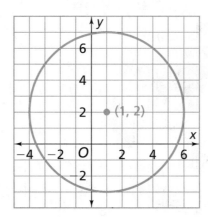

Find or estimate the missing coordinates for these points on the circle. In each case, use the Pythagorean Theorem to check that the point is 5 units from the center.

a. (■, 6) **b.** (5, ■) **c.** (−3, ■)

d. (1, ■) **e.** (■, 2) **f.** (4, ■)

46. This circle has radius 5 and center (1, 2). Segment *AC* is parallel to the *x*-axis. Segment *BC* is parallel to the *y*-axis.

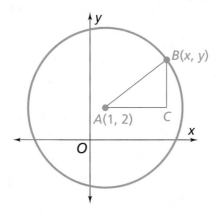

a. What are the lengths of segments *AC*, *BC*, and *AB* in terms of *x* and *y*?

b. What equation shows how these side lengths are related?

c. Suppose you redraw the figure with *B*(*x*, *y*) in a different position, but still on the circle. Would the coordinates of point *B* still fit the equation you wrote in part (b)?

d. Based on this Exercise, what do you think is the general equation for points on a circle with center (*m*, *n*) and radius *r*?

Mathematical Reflections 5

In this Investigation, you applied the ideas from the first three Investigations. The following questions will help you summarize what you have learned.

Think about these questions. Discuss your ideas with other students and your teacher. Then write a summary of your findings in your notebook.

1. **Give** at least two examples of ways in which the Pythagorean Theorem can be useful.

2. **Describe** the special properties of a 30-60-90 triangle.

3. **What** information do you need to write the equation of a circle with a center at the origin?

Common Core Mathematical Practices

As you worked on the Problems in this Investigation, you used prior knowledge to make sense of them. You also applied Mathematical Practices to solve the Problems. Think back over your work, the ways you thought about the Problems, and how you used Mathematical Practices.

Nick described his thoughts in the following way:

In Problem 5.2, we noticed that equilateral triangles have reflectional symmetry. So we could draw a vertical line from a vertex to the base opposite the vertex.

Once we divided the triangle into two separate triangles, we recognized which angles and sides were important and how they related to other parts of the triangle. We were then able to use this information and the Pythagorean Theorem to find the perimeter and area of the triangle.

Common Core Standards for Mathematical Practice

MP4 Model with mathematics.

 • What other Mathematical Practices can you identify in Nick's reasoning?

• Describe a Mathematical Practice that you and your classmates used to solve a different Problem in this Investigation.

While working on the Problems in this Unit, you extended your skill in using coordinate systems to locate points and figures. Then, by studying patterns in the side lengths and areas of squares on coordinate grids, you learned the Pythagorean Theorem for right triangles. You used that property of right triangles to solve a variety of practical problems, some of which involved irrational numbers.

Use Your Understanding: The Pythagorean Theorem

Test your understanding of the Pythagorean Theorem by solving the following problems.

1. The diagram below shows a Chinese tangram puzzle on a 10-by-10 grid.

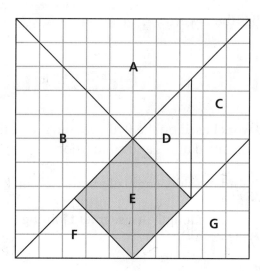

    a. What is the area of Shape E?

    b. What is the length of each side of Shape E?

    c. What are the lengths of the sides of Triangle A?

    d. Name all the triangles that are similar to Triangle A. In each case, give a scale factor for the similarity relationship.

2. A 60-foot piece of wire is strung between the top of a tower and the ground, making a 30-60-90 triangle.

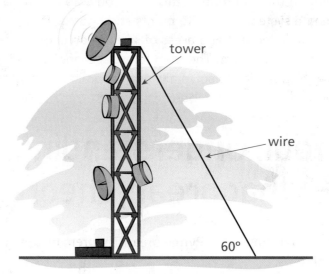

    a. How far from the center of the base of the tower is the wire attached to the ground?

    b. How high is the tower?

Explain Your Reasoning

When you present work based on the Pythagorean relationship, you should be able to justify your calculations and conclusions.

    3. How can you find the side length of a square if you know its area?

    4. How can you find the length of a segment joining two points on a coordinate grid?

5. The diagrams below show squares on the sides of triangles.

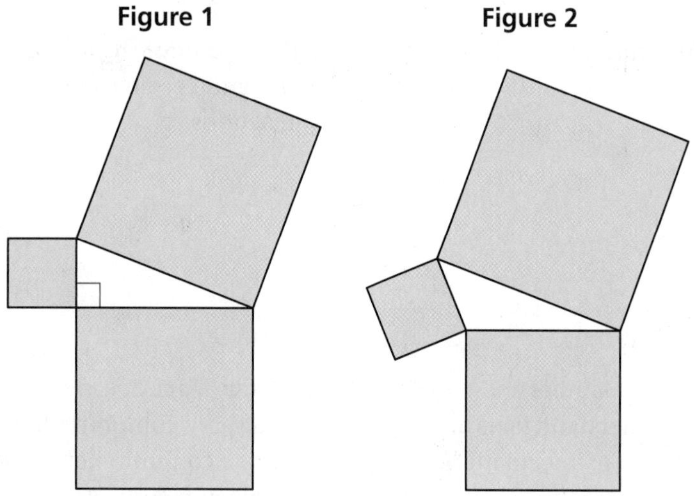

Figure 1   **Figure 2**

   a. In Figure 1, what is the relationship among the areas of the squares?

   b. Explain why the relationship you described in part (a) is not true for Figure 2.

6. Explain with words and symbols how to use the Pythagorean Theorem to find the following:

   a. the length of a diagonal of a square with side length s.

   b. the length of a diagonal of a rectangle with side lengths s and t.

   c. the length of the hypotenuse of a right triangle with legs of lengths s and t.

   d. the height of an equilateral triangle with side length s.

   e. the length of one leg of a triangle when the lengths of the hypotenuse and the other leg are h and t, respectively.

English / Spanish Glossary

A   **acute triangle**   An acute triangle is a triangle with three acute angles.

triángulo acutángulo   Un triángulo acutángulo es un triángulo cuyos tres ángulos son agudos.

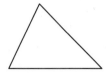

analyze   Academic Vocabulary
To think about and understand facts and details about a given set of information. Analyzing can involve providing a written summary supported by factual information, a diagram, chart, table, or a combination of these.

related terms   *explain, describe, justify*

sample   Analyze the squares. How is the side length of a square related to the area?

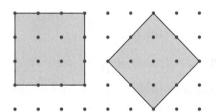

The first square has an area of 9 units^2 and a side length of 3 units. The side length is the square root of the area. The second square has an area of 4 full units^2 and 8 half-units^2 for a total of 8 units^2. The side length is the square root of the area or $\sqrt{8}$ units.

analizar   Vocabulario académico
Pensar para comprender datos y detalles sobre un conjunto determinado de información dada. Analizar puede incluir un resumen escrito apoyado por información real, un diagrama, una gráfica, una tabla o una combinación de estos.

términos relacionados   *explicar, describir, justificar*

ejemplo   Analiza los cuadrados. ¿Cómo se relaciona la longitud del lado con el área?

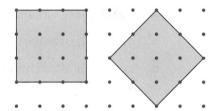

El primer cuadrado tiene un área de 9 unidades^2 y una longitud del lado de 3 unidades. La longitud del lado es la raíz cuadrada del área. El segundo cuadrado tiene un área de 4 unidades^2 completas y 8 unidades^2 medias que hacen un total de 8 unidades^2. La longitud del lado es la raíz cuadrada del área o $\sqrt{8}$ unidades.

C **cube root** If $A = s^3$, then s is the cube root of A. For example, 2 is the cube root of 8 because $2 \cdot 2 \cdot 2 = 8$. The $\sqrt[3]{}$ symbol is used to denote the cube root.

raíz cúbica Si $A = s^3$, entonces s es la raíz cúbica de A. Por ejemplo, 2 es la raíz cúbica de 8 porque $2 \cdot 2 \cdot 2 = 8$. El símbolo $\sqrt[3]{}$ se usa para indicar la raíz cúbica.

This cube has the volume of 8 cubic units. The length of each edge is the cube root of 8 units, which is equal to 2 units.

Este cubo tiene un volumen de 8 unidades cúbicas. La longitud de cada arista es la raíz cúbica de 8 unidades, que es igual a 2 unidades.

E **estimate** Academic Vocabulary
To find an approximate answer.

related terms *approximate, guess*

sample Estimate $\sqrt{10}$.

hacer una estimación Vocabulario académico Hallar una respuesta aproximada.

términos relacionados *aproximar, suponer*

ejemplo Estima $\sqrt{10}$.

I know that $\sqrt{9} = 3$ and $\sqrt{16} = 4$. Since $\sqrt{10}$ is much closer to $\sqrt{9}$ than it is to $\sqrt{16}$, my estimate will be closer to 3 than to 4. I tried 3.1, but $3.1^2 < 10$. I tried 3.2, but $3.2^2 > 10$. I estimate $\sqrt{10}$ as about 3.2.

Sé que $\sqrt{9} = 3$ y $\sqrt{16} = 4$. Puesto que $\sqrt{10}$ está mucho más cerca de $\sqrt{9}$ que de $\sqrt{16}$, mi estimación estaría más cercana a 3 que a 4. Intenté con 3.1, pero $3.1^2 < 10$. Intenté con 3.2, pero $3.2^2 > 10$. Estimo que $\sqrt{10}$ es aproximadamente 3.2.

F **find** Academic Vocabulary To use the given information and any related facts to determine or calculate a value. You may use mathematical algorithms, properties, formulas, or a combination of these, as well as other mathematical strategies, when finding a value.

related terms *calculate, discover, determine*

sample Find the area of the triangle below.

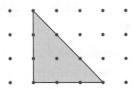

> I can count the number of unit squares. △ABC has an area of 4.5 unit squares. I can also find the area by using the formula $A = \frac{1}{2}bh$, where the base and the height of the triangle are each 3 units in length.
> $A = \frac{1}{2}(3)(3) = 4.5$ square units

hallar Vocabulario académico Usar la información dada y los datos relacionados para determinar o calcular un valor. Puedes usar algoritmos matemáticos, propiedades, fórmulas o una combinación de estos, así como otras estrategias matemáticas, cuando hallas un valor.

términos relacionados *calcular, descubrir, determinar*

ejemplo Halla el área del triángulo.

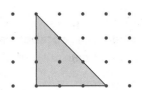

> Puedo contar ei número de unidades cuadradas. El △ABC tiene un área de 4.5 unidades cuadradas. Puedo hallar el área usando la fórmula $A = \frac{1}{2}ba$, donde la base y la altura del triángulo miden 3 unidades de longitud respectivamente.
> $A = \frac{1}{2}(3)(3) = 4.5$ unidades cuadradas

H hypotenuse The side of a right triangle that is opposite the right angle. The hypotenuse is the longest side of a right triangle. In the triangle below, the side labeled c is the hypotenuse.

hipotenusa El lado de un triángulo rectángulo que está opuesto al ángulo recto. La hipotenusa es el lado más largo de un triángulo rectángulo. En el triángulo de abajo, el lado rotulado c es la hipotenusa.

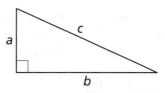

I irrational number A number that cannot be written as a quotient of two integers where the denominator is not 0. The decimal representation of an irrational number never ends and never shows a repeating pattern of a fixed number of digits. The numbers $\sqrt{2}$, $\sqrt{3}$, $\sqrt{5}$, and π are examples of irrational numbers.

número irracional Un número que no se puede escribir como el cociente de dos números enteros donde el denominador no es 0. La representación decimal de un número irracional nunca termina, y nunca muestra un patrón de un número fijo de dígitos que se repite. Los números $\sqrt{2}$, $\sqrt{3}$, $\sqrt{5}$, y π son ejemplos de números irracionales.

L legs The sides of a right triangle that are adjacent to the right angle. In the triangle above, the sides labeled a and b are legs.

catetos Los lados de un triángulo rectángulo que son adyacentes al ángulo recto. En el triángulo de arriba, los lados a y b son los catetos.

observe Academic Vocabulary

To notice or to examine carefully one or more characteristics of a particular object.

related terms *notice, examine, note, see*

sample What do you observe about the sum of the squares of the lengths of the legs of the right triangle in relationship to the length of the hypotenuse?

If I square the length of the hypotenuse, I get $5^2 = 25$. This is equal to the sum of the squares of the lengths of the legs of the triangle $3^2 + 4^2 = 9 + 16 = 25$.

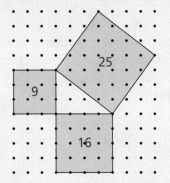

The area of the square built on the hypotenuse is equal to the sum of the areas of the squares built on the two legs of the right triangle.

observar Vocabulario académico

Notar o examinar con cuidado una o más características de un objeto determinado.

términos relacionados *notar, examinar, mirar, ver*

ejemplo ¿Qué observas sobre la suma de los cuadrados de las longitudes de los catetos del triángulo rectángulo con relación a la longitud de la hipotenusa?

Si elevo al cuadrado la longitud de la hipotenusa, obtengo $5^2 = 25$. Esto es igual a la suma de los cuadrados de las longitudes de los catetos del triángulo $3^2 + 4^2 = 9 + 16 = 25$.

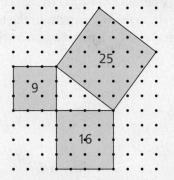

El área del cuadrado construido sobre la hipotenusa es igual a la suma de las áreas de los cuadrados construidos sobre los dos catetos del triángulo rectángulo.

obtuse triangle An obtuse triangle has one angle with a measure greater than 90°.

triángulo obtusángulo Un triángulo obtusángulo tiene un ángulo con una medida mayor que 90°.

P **perpendicular** Forming a right angle. For example, the sides of a right triangle that form the right angle are perpendicular.

perpendicular Que forma un ángulo recto. Por ejemplo, los lados de un triángulo rectángulo que forman el ángulo recto son perpendiculares.

Pythagorean Theorem A statement about the relationship among the lengths of the sides of a right triangle. The theorem states that if a and b are the lengths of the legs of a right triangle and c is the length of the hypotenuse, then $a^2 + b^2 = c^2$.

teorema de Pitágoras Un enunciado acerca de la relación que existe entre las longitudes de los lados de un triángulo rectángulo. El teorema enuncia que si a y b son las longitudes de los catetos de un triángulo rectángulo y c es la longitud de la hipotenusa, entonces $a^2 + b^2 = c^2$.

R **radius** A radius of a circle is the distance from the center of the circle to any point on the circle.

radio El radio de un círculo es la distancia que hay desde el centro del círculo a cualquier punto en el círculo.

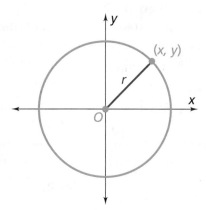

rational number A number that can be written as a quotient of two integers where the denominator is not 0. The decimal representation of a rational number either ends or repeats. Examples of rational numbers are $\frac{1}{2}$, $\frac{80}{99}$, 7, 0.2, and 0.191919 . . .

número racional Un número que se puede escribir como el cociente de dos números enteros donde el denominador no es 0. La representación decimal de un número racional termina o se repite. Ejemplos de números racionales son $\frac{1}{2}$, $\frac{80}{99}$, 7, 0.2 y 0.191919 . . .

real numbers The set of all rational numbers and all irrational numbers. The number line represents the set of real numbers.

números reales El conjunto de todos los números racionales y todos los números irracionales. La recta numérica representa el conjunto de los números reales.

....

repeating decimal A decimal with a pattern of a fixed number of digits that repeats forever, such as 0.3333333 . . . and 0.73737373 . . . . Repeating decimals are rational numbers.

decimal periódico Un número decimal con un patrón de un número fijo de dígitos que se repite infinitamente, como 0.3333333 . . . y 0.73737373 . . . Los decimales que se repiten son números racionales.

....

right triangle A right triangle is a triangle with one right angle.

triángulo rectángulo Un triángulo rectángulo es un triángulo que tiene un ángulo recto.

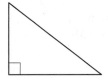

....

S **square root** If $A = s^2$, then s is the square root of A. For example, -3 and 3 are square roots of 9 because $3 \cdot 3 = 9$ and $-3 \cdot (-3) = 9$. The $\sqrt{\ }$ symbol is used to denote the positive square root. So, you write $\sqrt{9} = 3$. The positive square root of a number is the side length of a square that has that number as its area.

raíz cuadrada Si $A = s^2$, entonces s es la raíz cuadrada de A. Por ejemplo, -3 y 3 son raíces cuadradas de 9 porque $3 \cdot 3 = 9$ y $-3 \cdot (-3) = 9$. El símbolo $\sqrt{\ }$ se usa para indicar la raíz cuadrada positiva. Por eso, escribimos $\sqrt{9} = 3$. La raíz cuadrada positiva de un número es la longitud del lado de un cuadrado que tiene dicho número como su área.

....

T **terminating decimal** A decimal that ends, or terminates, such as 0.5 or 0.125. Terminating decimals are rational numbers.

decimal finito Un decimal que se acaba o termina, como 0.5 ó 0.125. Los decimales finitos son números racionales.

....

theorem A theorem is a general mathematical statement that has been proven true.

teorema Un teorema es un enunciado matemático general que se ha demostrado.

Index

Acknowledgments

Cover Design

Three Communication Design, Chicago

Text

084 Excerpt from "*The Wizard of Oz*" granted courtesy of Warner Bros. Entertainment Inc, ©1939. All Rights Reserved.

Photographs

Photo locators denoted as follows: Top (T), Center (C), Bottom (B), Left (L), Right (R), Background (Bkgd)

002 (CR) Erich Lessing/Art Resource, NY, (BR) David R. Frazier Photolibrary, Inc./Alamy; **003** Hfng/Shutterstock; **007** Encyclopedia/Corbis; **041** Getty Images/Thinkstock; **046** Erich Lessing/Art Resource, NY; **079** David R. Frazier Photolibrary, Inc./Alamy; **081** S.F. Hess California League/Baseball Cards/Library of Congress Prints and Photographs Division; **084** Warner Bros/Everett Collection, Inc.; **096** Huw Jones/Lonely Planet Images/Getty Images.